Praise for
The Sugar Addict' ███████

WITHDRAWN

"People are desperate to find the answer . . . whoever said *'You can't have your cake and eat it too?'* The time has come!"

Mary Jane
Entrepreneur
Bradenton, Florida

"By following this program I lost 10 lbs. in the first two weeks and, after five months, I'm up to 20 lbs! Also, I was taking the prescribed medication, Klonopin, 2 to 3 times a day for recurring panic attacks. By replacing white flour products with whole grain options (especially pasta), quitting caffeine, and eliminating the major sources of sugar in my diet, I have been able to go completely off this medication.

What I like best about S. J.'s diet is that it is simple and easy to find satisfying substitutes whenever I have a sugar craving."

Juanita
Teacher
Sarasota, Florida

"Nicotine. Sugar. Deadly addictive substances. *The Sugar Addict's Diet* gives you practical easy ways to reclaim your personal power. I've gotten my life back!"

Dr. Elaine Onofrey
Acupuncture Physician
Holmes Beach, Florida

Funding for this g
the Illinois State Library, a Division of
the Office of Secretary of State, using
federal LSTA funding.

"Before an individual is given prescription drugs to lower anxiety levels [or] to bring them up from depression or control their anger, their dietary habits should be assessed. It is frightening that so many of our children are on medication to control their behavior, why not consider a less risky option first?

I highly recommend this book to everyone and especially to doctors, counselors, and others who treat the physical and psychological illnesses that may have been brought on by too much sugar in the diet. We owe it to our patients and our clients to know how this *drug* can adversely affect their lives."

Susan Bierker, MSW, ACSW
Psychotherapist
Siesta Key, Florida

"I've tried other diets, and even lost weight, but was never able to keep it off because as soon as I went back to *normal* eating the weight came back. *The Sugar Addict's Diet* is not about deviating from regular eating patterns. Therefore, it is something I can stick with long term. It is a healthful way of life for anyone, not just people with a weakness for sugar."

Valeri
Accountant
Seattle, Washington

"S. J. is an extremely credible writer. I have seen improvements in my health and fitness where I did not believe improvement was possible and weight *control* is no longer a mystery."

Greg
Photographer
Salt Lake City, Utah

The
Sugar Addict's Diet

A Primer for the Low Sugar Lifestyle

A Path of Healing, Wellness, and Weight Loss

S. J. Wise

with a foreword by Estaban Genao, M.D.
and Susan Bierker, MSW, ACSW

New Century Publishing 2000

Not all diets are suitable for everyone and this or any other diet program may result in variable success. Any user of this program assumes responsibility for the weight loss and health obtained. The author, publisher, and distributors of this book do not specifically endorse any of the products listed nor do they make any claim that these products or their ingredients are healthful. Not all products listed are safe for diabetics or hypoglycemics. Products may be high in fat or contain ingredients such as aspartame, polyols, or hydrogenated oils that may be hazardous to your health. To reduce risk of health, consult your doctor before beginning this program. This book is not intended to replace medical advice or be a substitute for a physician. If you are taking prescribed medication please consult your physician as any dietary changes will affect the metabolism of that medication. The creators, contributors, and distributors of this program expressly disclaim responsibility for any adverse effects, liabilities, or loss in connection with the advice herein.

THE SUGAR ADDICT'S DIET

PUBLISHING HISTORY
New Century Publishing 2000. Soft cover edition published March 2001.

ISBN 0-9701110-5-3

Cover Design: Janine White
Cover photo: Digital Imagery © 2001 Photodisc, Inc.
Library of Congress Catalog Card Number: 00-112293

For information contact:
New Century Publishing 2000
U.S.A. - P.O. Box 36, East Canaan, CT 06024 (888) 217-7233
CANADA - 60 Bullock Dr., Unit 6, Markham ON L3P 3P2   (905) 471-5711

About the Author

S. J. Wise has a colorful and varied background. She has worked as a surgical nurse, karate instructor, free lance artist, and stand-up comic sharing the stage with both Roseanne Barr and Jenny Jones.

As a surgical scrub nurse, S. J. had first-hand experience with the downside of weight gain. She performed stomach stapling, liposuction, breast augmentation, and "tummy tucks"; often physically carrying pounds of fat away from the OR table. She was involved in many surgeries in which the patient's illness was obesity related. These included cancer, tumors and scores of amputations as a result of diabetes. S. J. acquired her nursing training while on active duty in the U.S. Army during Desert Storm. She has a degree in surgical technology and attended the University of Utah in Salt Lake City.

She has been part of the fitness industry since 1973 when she began her martial arts training. In 1977 Sabina went to Japan to study at the world famous Karate University of Nichidai in Tokyo. At 15 she was Utah State Sparring Champion, acquiring that title twice, Colorado Champion in 1979, and the Southwestern U.S. Champion in 1988. She is now a 5th degree black belt, certified through the Japan International Karate Do Association and the American Federation of Ju Jitsu, holding rank in three different styles of the martial arts. She has trained with Bill "Superfoot" Wallace, Ed Parker (founder of the Kenpo style in America), and Chuck Norris as a judge in the USA World Championships in Las Vegas in 1994. She was Children's Self Defense Coordinator for America's Safety Awareness Program and past president of The Women's Karate Association of Utah.

Her search for the most ideal form of physical fitness training led her to yoga. She has been a yoga practitioner for more than twelve years, completing courses in the Iyengar, Kripalu, Sivananda, Kundalini, and Ashtanga styles. She currently teaches her own course of instruction.

As a published artist and writer for more than twenty years, S. J.'s credits include *Healthy & Natural Journal, The Event Magazine, Survival Magazine*, medical textbook illustrations, and a CD cover design for Aida House Records.

Born on the border of France and Germany, S. J. presently resides with her family in Florida.

To my husband
for encouraging me to embark upon a path of *self education*
that resulted in profound *self-healing*,

and to all those who have suffered
for so long without an advocate.

Acknowledgments

My sincere thanks to Deb Gorham, former Editor of *Healthy & Natural Magazine*, for setting me on the right path. I am grateful to Nina Anderson, of New Century Publishing 2000, for her strong encouragement and positive attitude; and also to Dr. Howard Peiper, co-author of *The Secrets of Staying Young*, for his personal comments and suggestions.

A special thanks to Suza Francina, author of *The New Yoga for People Over 50* and Mayor of Ojai, California, for her cheerful and enthusiastic support, and also for her significant efforts to educate our community about this very serious issue.

Thank you, Susan Bierker, for enriching my life (and the lives of so many others!) in countless ways. Your kind spirit and generosity have added much to this work. God bless.

My gratitude to Dr. Estaban Genao, renowned south Florida pediatrician, for sharing his valuable time in writing the inspiring foreword to this book, and Dr. Harold Tabaie for taking time out of his busy schedule, as a cardiovascular surgeon, to critique my manuscript. Warm and gracious thanks to Clif and the wonderful folks at Good Earth Natural Foods for their contribution to this project, my kitchen, and to our city.

The depth of gratitude I feel for Mr. William Dufty can hardly be expressed in words. His book *Sugar Blues* brought tears to my eyes as it awakened me to the negative impact of refined sugar on our global community. His book marked a turning point in my life. He is a pioneer in this work and I cannot thank him enough as I attempt to carry on his anti-sugar legacy.

Let me also express my appreciation for the folks at Westbay, for their enduring support . . . my yogis and friends; my Namaste' group–I couldn't have managed without you; and so many others whose friendship has been invaluable—Valeri Nebeker, Marli, Nancy, Donise, Amy (my number one fan!), Janice, Elaine, and Steve. And, of course, my family for pushing me out of the nest.

One more, very significant, word of thanks goes out to all the healthcare workers around the world who, despite contempt from their peers, have cared enough to educate themselves and their patients about good nutrition in the role of healing.

To Write to the Author

If you experience positive changes due to a low sugar diet, have a story of hope and healing that you would like to share, or would like to schedule a speaking engagement, please write to the author in care of this publisher. We cannot guarantee that every letter can be answered, but all will be forwarded. Please enclose a self-addressed stamped envelope or $2.00 to cover costs.

S. J. Wise
c/o New Century Publishing 2000
60 Bullock Dr. Unit 6, Markham, ON LP3 3P2

or email:
wisearts@yahoo.com

Preface

A whopping 97 million Americans from ages 20 to 74 are either overweight or obese. That's a little more than half of all adults from coast to coast. On any given day, a full one-quarter of all overweight men and half of all overweight women, some eighty million Americans, are on a diet. Many of these people try one diet after another for years at a time. Are you one of these?

Perhaps you've developed a pattern of gaining weight during the winter months and then going on a crash diet to fit into your bathing suit each spring; or you lose weight with one diet but eventually give it up. Then you gain back the weight you lost, plus a few additional pounds, and are soon looking for the next new diet.

How would you like to get off the diet roller coaster forever? This book contains a simple weight control formula that will allow you to do just that. Cutting refined sugar from your diet is also a way to cut fat. No more counting fat grams or calories. Best of all, with the delicious products and recipes outlined, you won't even feel deprived.

Western medicine has been slow to recognize the severity of the refined sugar problem and has even, in some cases, given false nutritional advice as in the case of this author. After developing Graves Disease, a thyroid disorder, S. J. Wise sought medical treatment and was told that eating sugar to combat her resultant hypoglycemia was "not a problem." This advice only helped to exacerbate her condition.

The medical community encouraged her to take drugs and to have surgery; both of which she was adamantly against. She was finally forced to quit her career as a surgical nurse due to her disease symptoms. Only after the encouragement of her husband, who believes in self-education and the holistic approach, did she begin to get well. S. J. achieved remission of her disease without surgery or radiation. She accomplished this by adhering to a sugar-free diet. The principle of low sugar eating was a regimen that was easy to follow and it gave her, for the first time in her life, the power to control her weight as well as her health.

In *The Sugar Addict's Diet* S. J. shares some of her favorite low sugar products with you; the products that allowed her to continue to eat in the manner that she was accustomed (luscious treats, ice cream, and even chocolate) but without harming her health or her weight. You too, can benefit from the low sugar lifestyle: a path of healing, wellness, and weight loss without the deprivation of dieting.

* * * * *

The low sugar lifestyle is not a "diet." It is just what it implies: a way of life. There is no such thing as cheating, because the only regimen involved is replacing your favorite high sugar foods with lower sugar versions whenever you can. If you cannot do this (for instance, at a family gathering), it's all right. Just start again when you get home. There are no ill effects to cutting sugar. And in the long run even a small reduction can reap great health rewards. But do keep in mind that sugar is similar to a drug (see Chapter One) and if withdrawal is not gradual you might experience some side effects, as with any long-term toxic habit.

Deprivation is unnecessary. You don't have to *feel* like you are on a diet. This book includes everything from chocolate and ice cream to hot fudge sundaes. But it explains how you can choose the healthier options; how you can eat these foods without gaining weight or harming your health. The author has learned how to do this for herself. She is living the low sugar lifestyle. She has gone from a size 14 to a size 6 and is in remission from disease. The low sugar lifestyle works!

> "She has gone from a size 14 to a size 6 and is in remission from disease."

As a consumer, choosing to follow the low sugar path may also save you money. It is not necessary to pay for expensive diet programs or supplements. This book contains the information that will set you free of other, more exploitative, programs in the diet industry.

Now is the time to make a commitment to a new way of life. But also take a moment to consider the other people in your life. Can you be instrumental in improving the lives of those you love as well? What would you do with the added energy of four more hours in every day? Are your children overactive? Do they lack concentration? The benefits of reducing sugar consumption are much more than just preventing cavities. Some of these benefits include increased clarity, energy, concentration, productivity, relief of migraine headaches, insomnia, anxiety attacks, and sexual dysfunction. Of course, you will keep your teeth a little longer but how about a boost to your immune system as well.

When you discover the positive changes in your own life, why not be an advocate for low sugar living? Share this message with your loved ones and friends. You may not only *change* a life, you may *save* a life.

Table of Contents

Foreword

C andy and other sugary treats are often given to children as a reward for good behavior. I am amazed and *terrified* to see such a common practice in our society today. I agree wholeheartedly with S. J. that sugar is an addictive drug. It has a toxic and drugging affect on the human body.

When we consume sugar in any shape or form, in food, in candy, or in liquids it ferments in the digestive system causing the formation of acetic acid, carbonic acid, and alcohol. Acetic acid is a powerfully destructive acid. It causes serious damage to the delicate membranes in the intestinal tract, literally burning the cells. And because of its affinity for the fats in the nervous tissue, it reacts on the nerves with a paralyzing effect.

The alcohol created by sugar in the system is equally destructive, causing reactions similar in behavior to beverage alcohol, even to the extent of violent reactions. It tends to gradually destroy the texture of the kidneys. It also affects the nerves, which are closely related to the brain, thereby disrupting the functions of observation, concentration, and locomotion – in the same manner that alcoholic beverages do.

Refined sugar or sucrose is a man-made chemical, truly a dangerous drug. People who consume sugar will eventually experience the same degeneration as a drug addict. With sugar as addictive as morphine, most people experience a strong craving for more after just one taste. In Chapter One of *The Sugar Addict's Diet,* S. J. Wise addresses this issue, a fact commonly overlooked by the food industry and medical community either by ignorance or because of economic gain.

Our children are born to sugar addiction. The average American begins consuming sugar shortly after birth as the nurse places a bottle of sugar water in the infant's mouth. It is common practice to add sugar to infant formula to make it more palatable. The commercial baby food industry also adds sugar to their processed food products because an infant's taste buds might otherwise reject these unnatural foods. Parents feed their children breakfast cereals, many of which contain in excess of fifty percent sugar. Then comes ice cream and refined carbohydrates such as cakes, candies, pies, soft drinks, and donuts. On top of all this there are many more hidden sources of refined sugar in foods that we presume are healthy. Some of these include catsup, peanut butter, fruit yogurt (as much as 49 grams per serving!), and fruit juice (even without added sugar, juice may contain as much as 40 grams of sugar per serving). And, that healthy bran muffin is loaded with added sugar.

Before a child reaches the age of one, so much sugar and refined carbohydrates have already been consumed that it will be almost impossible for that child to develop a normal functioning immune system. Hormonal production will be out of balance and the digestive system will be inefficient. There will be early disruption of pancreas, stomach, and liver function. A violation of the adrenal glands will result in faulty brain activity. Is it any wonder that children and adolescents today suffer frequent infections, perennial allergies, and so many behavioral problems?

Current studies reveal that consumption of refined sugar may be as high as 140 pounds per person per year with our children and young adolescents the primary target of the sugar industry. Sucrose in the diet has been shown to be one of the main causes of discipline problems with children, and it may be the root cause leading to alcoholism, crime, rape, murder, and a host of other social ills. After twenty years as a pediatrician I agree with the author that over-consumption of sugar may be the reason we have such a violent and unstable generation of young people today. Yes, indeed, many studies demonstrate that a poor, processed food diet, especially one high in sugar, can result in criminal behavior.

Children are not the only ones affected. Because sugar is a "dead" food it creates pancreatic disturbances that result in many serious ailments and afflictions. Probably two of the most severe are hypoglycemia and diabetes. Most people suffering from hypoglycemia are not even aware that they have it. Psychological problems resulting from hypoglycemia may cause a gamut of disturbances, not the least of which are irritability, depression, and upset with spouse and children for no apparent reason. Marriage counselors familiar with hypoglycemia estimate that up to fifty percent of all marriage problems can be traced to this condition.

I agree also with S. J. that the Western medical establishment has been slow to recognize the severity of this problem, often rejecting that a refined sugar problem even exists. Much of the medical community still claims that causes for some maladies are unknown and regularly prescribe drugs rather than dietary changes. In Chapter 3, S. J. presents a short but precise account of the ever-increasing problem of hypoglycemia. I highly recommend a careful reading of this chapter because I believe that symptoms of low blood sugar today are almost universally present in any person who consumes refined carbohydrates.

The physiology of the human body cannot be ignored. There are biochemical pathways that we must respect. Claiming ignorance will not save us from suffering. The word sugar creates confusion. Sugar is very important in the function of metabolism. There is always sugar present in the blood stream, known as blood glucose, and this is an essential component of the human system. There are also sugars in nature. Fruits give us simple sugars while grains give us sugar in the form of starches or complex carbohydrates. When we consume natural sugar its fiber allows the sugar to enter the blood stream in a slow steady flow; more importantly, the presence of micronutrients, such as the B-complex vitamins and minerals, permit an efficient conversion of this sugar into energy, the primary reason that we eat.

Let's take just a moment to examine the effects of consuming white sugar. Weight gain: just drinking one twelve-ounce can of cola or soda a day will add 12 pounds of weight to the body in a year. It upsets mineral balance creating symptoms and, ultimately, disease: white sugar or sucrose leaches "B" vitamins from the body, creating a myriad of metabolic problems; it destroys calcium and depletes the body of magnesium and many essential trace minerals, mainly chromium and zinc. All these "B" vitamins are essential for the conversion of foodstuff into energy. The lack of any of them will make it impossible for a person to function normally at any level. This clearly demonstrates that the solution is not another drug but rather, as elegantly stated in this book, a *food cure*.

Sugar, as glucose, is the principle fuel that the muscles and other portions of the body consume to produce energy. It is present in every cell and almost every fluid of the body, and its concentration and distribution are among the most important processes in human physiology. We need to consume healthy carbohydrates but we do not need refined processed white sugar in our diets. How can we begin to choose more wisely? Reading *The Sugar Addict's Diet* is the first step.

I highly recommend *The Sugar Addict's Diet* as a stepping stone toward better health. I am already applying this book in my personal life and medical practice. As a pediatrician I am always trying to convince my patients to break the sugar habit. Now, with the help of this book, this work is becoming much easier. Ms. Wise gives us so many resources that surely you will find the means to overcome the single most urgent problem in America today, refined sugar addiction.

I will close by confessing that I also was a sugar addict. Fortunately, I was able to find a healthy solution to this problem by using a sugar substitute. My favorite, and the only supplement I use for sweetening food, is Stevia (as detailed in Chapter 1). I believe it is the best option available today. My hope is that one day it will be the only sweetener used in any diet product.

Estaban Genao, M.D.
Pediatrician
Miami, Florida

* * * * * * *

In my twenty years as a psychotherapist in Pennsylvania and three years as a counselor in Florida, I have treated many clients who are so anxious that they have difficulty functioning in life. Some are so depressed that they are frozen into immobility, feeling hopeless, and even suicidal. Many experience inordinately large mood swings. Others exhibit rage that is so overwhelming that it wreaks havoc in their marriages, jobs, and other parts of their lives.

I was amazed to read how much sugar each individual in this country eats on the average. The children of many of my clients are often on medication to calm them down, which leads me to believe that the entire family may be overdosing on sugar.

I am not suggesting that every emotional issue that a person has is due to a sugar addiction. However, I strongly believe that sugar consumption needs to be considered as a possible cause of the problem. Before an individual is given prescription drugs to lower anxiety levels or even out mood swings, to bring them up from the depths of depression or control their anger, their dietary habits should be assessed. It is frightening that so many of our society's children are on medication to control their behavior, especially hyperactivity. These medications are valuable if they are truly needed but why not consider a less risky option first?

S. J. Wise has written a most valuable book. It is for those who are unaware of the effects of sugar, but even more so, for those who cannot seem to reduce their sugar intake because of their severe sugar addiction. I, personally, have known for many years that sugar consumption may be harmful, but after reading this book, I found that it was even more damaging than I had imagined to so many aspects of psychological and physical health. It was a real eye-opener! Sugar is a drug with absolutely no redeeming virtues.

Fortunately for the reader, S. J. tells us what to do about the issue of sugar addiction. Guidance is given on how to cut down on the more harmful sugars and how to satisfy our sweet cravings with natural sweeteners that are less dangerous. And to add frosting to the cake, delicious product replacements are offered that will satisfy even the most hardened sugar addict.

I highly recommend this book to everyone and especially to doctors, counselors, and others who treat the physical and psychological illnesses that may have been brought on by too much sugar in the diet. We owe it to our patients and our clients to know how this *drug* can adversely affect their lives.

Susan Bierker, MSW, ACSW
Psychotherapist
Siesta Key, Florida

Introduction

High protein diets are being recognized as potentially harmful while low sugar diets are on the upswing. Why? High protein diets are based on the principle of ketosis. Without enough incoming carbohydrates, the body will first burn its limited carbohydrate stores, and then the protein in its lean muscle tissue, both of which release a great deal of water. Your body begins burning fat, but in an inefficient way that creates toxic by-products called ketones. These build up in the blood stream and must be processed through the kidneys to be eliminated.

This is an unhealthy state that may result in dizziness, headaches, mental confusion, nausea, fatigue, insomnia, and bad breath. High protein intake also causes the body to lose calcium, resulting in weakening of the bones. If this isn't bad enough, some of these diets encourage you to assuage hunger by ingesting red meat (including bacon), eggs (including the yolks), cream instead of milk, mayonnaise, fried food, and rich sugar-laden desserts! These are foods that promote the development of atherosclerosis, as well as many other disease conditions.

In ketosis your body thinks it is starving, so it will slow your metabolism down to conserve fuel and it will begin to eat the muscle tissue to get at the carbohydrates stored there as glycogen. Over time this condition can lead to severe problems including kidney damage.

Not only is it difficult to eliminate carbohydrates from your diet, but should you manage to do so you will eventually gain the weight back that you lose once you stop the diet. Your body will fight to turn everything you eat into fat because it doesn't know when you will be starving again. Of course, this ultimately results in more fat than when you began.

With *The Sugar Addict's Diet* you don't need to give up your favorite carbohydrate foods. Merely replace them with the absolutely delicious (and sweet!) low sugar, and often low fat, alternatives.

In this book you will find healthier replacements for such things as cookies, ice cream, chocolates, and even hot fudge sundaes! But you will also find the best yogurts, cereals, energy bars, and even chocolate milk.

You will be able to make healthier choices. Cutting down on sugar is difficult. These "replacement foods" will leave you feeling less deprived and will prove to you, once and for all, that diet success is possible.

In addition, most diets also promote vigorous daily aerobic exercise; a regimen that is clearly not for everyone. Although aerobic exercise is recommended for fitness, if you are one of the many people that cannot maintain a daily aerobic fitness program (which is most of us) you can rest assured that increased health and weight loss may be achieved through an improved diet alone. Remember, cutting sugar also means a reduction in fat and calories. The renewed energy that you discover may also be the impetus for you to start an exercise program. Certainly you will be burning more calories just by being more active in your day to day affairs.

With *The Sugar Addict's Diet* there is no strenuous fitness routine that must be adhered to for the weight loss program. This is particularly helpful for those who are not of an athletic temperament. Studies have shown that over-exercise such as intense aerobics or kickboxing at a calorie-burning rate of up to 800 calories per hour may actually inhibit fat burning. This kind of workout may lead to an anaerobic condition where energy is drawn from the muscles rather than from fat stores. The best exercise for fat burning is a slow, sustained low-metabolism workout. If you are utterly sedentary at present, do consider starting a minimal program of walking, yoga, tai chi, armchair or water aerobics. These fitness routines offer relief of stress in addition to enhanced weight loss. If you are intimidated by a classroom situation, then do as I did and try a book or videotape first. Check the resources section for further information on these programs.

If you are interested in yoga be aware that there are a full range of difficulty levels in the styles available. The Ashtanga style is geared to a more rigorous approach with students actually working up a sweat. Other styles such as Kripalu and Iyengar are more sedate and meditative. Check out several different classes to find the approach and instructor that is right for you. Exercise should include a warm-up stretch and a cool down period. It should be vigorous enough to elevate your heart rate, but not so intense that it is difficult to breathe or speak. Never allow yourself to be intimidated into moving at a pace that is beyond your fitness level.

I tell my yoga students to modify every exercise to meet their own individual health requirements. Rest when you feel like resting. If you are working at the edge of *your* capacity, but consistently, in time you will reach your fitness goals.

We must honor where our bodies are at, a condition that may change from day to day. We must never push or strain too hard. It is not necessary to *compete* with anyone, not even ourselves. But it is necessary to move, even if only a little. Recent studies have shown that diseases of aging are not linked to the passage of time at all. But rather, to inactivity.

Part I
Sugar and its Implications

Chapter 1
Sugar is a Drug

S uppose I were to describe a substance to you, by telling you that it comes as tiny white crystals, is highly refined, and once you try it you are "hooked" forever, what would you say it was? Cocaine? Crack? Methamphetamine? Would you be surprised to hear that the answer is simple table *sugar*?

In *Sugar Blues,* William Dufty describes sugar as a poison that is more lethal than opium. Sugar is only a chemical, he explains, in the same way that heroin is a chemical. From the juice of the poppy seed this "natural" substance is refined into opium, then morphine, and ultimately into heroin. Consider now the refinement process of sugar. The juice of the sugar cane or beet, evolves to molasses (a dark, sticky by-product); and from there to brown sugar (often confused as a healthier option but merely white sugar with added molasses or caramel coloring); then finally to the "strange white crystals" we find on our grocery store shelves, a product as addictive (and lethal!) as any illegal drug.

In fact, crystallized white sugar is a pharmaceutically pure chemical. The original food, that was whole and nutritious, has been stripped of all minerals, vitamins, enzymes, and amino acids (proteins). The same holds true for the refinement of white flour products. The vitamin-rich outer husk has been removed leaving only a fine white powder that has been bleached with toxic chemicals.

Why is this "food" so bad for us? The problem lies in the fact that, without its nutritional properties intact this now toxic substance must leach these nutrients from other areas of the body in order to be efficiently metabolized. Every time we consume white food we deplete our nutritional stores and we become less healthy, less whole. Eventually this strain takes its toll and a disease condition develops.

Reduce Slowly

If you don't think sugar is a drug, try to quit. Like any addictive drug, quitting sugar "cold turkey" is virtually impossible. Your body has adapted to this mal-nutrient. Reduce slowly. Educate yourself. Read as much as you can about this substance. Books such as *Sugar Blues* by William Dufty, *Lick the Sugar Habit* by Nancy Appleton, and *Sugar Busters!: Cut Sugar to Trim Fat* are a great place to start. If you have symptoms of some kind you might also want to read Dr. Paavo Airola's *Hypoglycemia: A Better Approach* and Dr. Harvey M. Ross and Jeraldine Saunders' *Hypoglycemia: The Disease Your Doctor Won't Treat*. It is possible that you might have undiagnosed (or even misdiagnosed) hypoglycemia. Check the bibliography for more informative reading.

Most of us don't think we eat a lot of sugar. Federal dietary guidelines suggest ten teaspoons of sugar a day as the maximum. But that is easily attained by the processed foods we eat with added sugars that we are not even aware of. Glucose, an ingredient as harmful as sugar, is commonly used by the food industry as a cheap filler and there are no laws requiring that it be listed on any label. Read *Lick The Sugar Habit* by Nancy Appleton, Ph.D., a food and nutrition expert. Her book explains, much better than I ever could, the connection between sugar consumption and the degenerative disease process.

So you say you have a treat only once in a while. Consider this: one-half of a large cola and one-half of a 7 oz. package of flavored licorice sticks (a typical movie theater snack) has about 77 cubes of added sugar! By switching to a diet cola (or better yet, bottled water!) and sugar-free licorice (See Chapter 6) you can save both your metabolic energy and your waistline.

> *"If you don't think sugar is a drug, try to quit."*

With sugar so culturally pervasive it is highly unlikely that you are naturally and easily sugar free. For most people cutting down is difficult and it may take several weeks before you get used to "normal" blood sugar levels, especially if you have had high blood sugar levels for some time. Try eating whole grains as they metabolize more slowly than white flour products. This will help reduce your sugar cravings. And as an added bonus, these foods allow you to increase the space between your meals resulting in fewer calories consumed. Of course, fewer calories means greater potential weight loss. I have found that if you can make it past the first three days, cravings for sugar and white flour items diminish and then ultimately disappear (until a holiday, of course). When I eat the "replacement foods," found in this book, it is because I want them not because I need them. I have a little taste and then I am done. Back in the days when I freely ate refined sugar products I was never *done*. One bite meant a binge. You may know what I mean. It was not uncommon for me to consume a whole carton of ice cream or even a whole pie (now there's a confession!). The non-sugar substitutes are free of this insidious side effect. You *can* eat just one. Hallelujah!

Why do we love sugar so much when it has no positive nutritional value? As a highly refined food product it has no vitamins, minerals, or dietary fiber. It has a tendency to lead us toward obesity, tooth decay, hypoglycemia, diabetes, and a whole slew of other ailments. It wreaks havoc with the body's metabolism. It even contributes to atherosclerosis. Unless you eat the food in its natural state there is no way to tell when you have had too much. The average American consumption of sugar is about two pounds a week and nearly three quarters of that is in the processed prepackaged food we buy.

The reason we crave sugar products is metabolic, not entirely psychological. Sure, therapy might help with some problems but I was greatly relieved to discover that my overeating compulsions could be brought under control by eliminating the main culprit: sugar. If you think that you overeat because you hate yourself, your body, your life, etc. try reducing your sugar consumption. Your symptoms of self-loathing might just disappear along with your cravings. In fact, sugar might be at the root of most of our cravings including alcoholism, tobacco, caffeine, and even drug addiction.

We must be informed of the detrimental side effects of sugar. Few even understand that they are addicted. In fact, most people still believe that sugar is relatively harmless. Sugar products, like any potential health hazard, should come with a warning label. Parents still reward their children with high sugar treats, ignorant of the very serious side effects they may be inflicting. Everyone knows that sugar promotes tooth decay but few are aware of the psychological damage related to sugar consumption: depression, mood swings, binge eating and its associated guilt, panic attacks, anxiety, paranoia, phobias, and even hallucinations to name a few. Sugar consumption can also contribute to the development and exacerbation of many major illnesses including heart disease, diabetes, and morbid obesity. Two studies, out of the Netherlands and Italy, now link sugar to the development of certain types of cancer as well.

Many people who have been "cured" through a sugar-free diet had actually been misdiagnosed at some point, often having been told that the symptoms were "all in their head." The erroneous diagnoses included such diverse conditions as mental retardation, Parkinson's syndrome, Psycho-neuroticism, cerebral arteriosclerosis, brain tumors, epilepsy, Compulsive Obsessive Disorder, Post Traumatic Stress Disorder, Attention Deficit Disorder, Social Phobia (up to ten million Americans diagnosed annu-ally!), acute paranoia, and even Schizophrenia.

Another popular misdiagnosis is rheumatoid arthritis. I was told I had this at age twenty-nine, but have had no more joint pain since reduc-ing the refined sugar in my diet. Actually, there is a link between hypogly-cemia and rheumatoid arthritis. A blood sugar imbalance may cause the adrenal glands to become overstimulated resulting in a reduction of corti-sone to the joints. This can ultimately cause joint damage, inflammation, and pain. Of course, I received no such explanation at the time of my di-agnosis. Nor did I receive any diet recommendations that might help.

> *"Stop blaming yourself. It is not your fault."*

As far as overeating was concerned I never knew that the food it-self was the culprit; that it was not just a matter of willpower. No one told me. But, I am here to tell you. Stop blaming yourself. It is not your fault. Sugar, just like any dangerous drug, will make you behave in ways that are beyond your control. What you need to do is learn how to control sugar. And, mind you, it's not easy to tame the sugar beast. I despise the creature but openly admit that I have not yet gone a full year without it. Like any addictive substance, it is charming and extremely seductive. The products in this book, though, have made my transition a little easier. They have literally saved my life and my sanity. Hopefully, they will help you as well.

When those moments of sugar weakness arise, you now have a re-source. First try to eat a substitute for the treat that you are craving. When eating out, it is easier to find sugar-free options than you might think. Of-ten buffet tables have a sugar-free section. If you don't see one, ask. Sometimes the sugar-free desserts are unmarked. But most restaurants have them. Don't be afraid to make an issue of it. We need to train our cu-linary establishments to meet our needs.

If you are unable to find a sugar-free replacement, and you simply must have something sweet, do try to eat your "real" treat or dessert at the end of a well-balanced meal high in protein. The American Diabetes Association suggests this as a way to help maintain your glucose balance. My own experience proves this to some extent. However, because sugar begets sugar, limit these episodes. In the same way that an alcoholic cannot take even one drink, so a sugarholic cannot eat his dessert without starting a craving cycle again. Whenever I cheat a little on a special occasion I find that it usually takes me a full week or two to cut back to zero sugar consumption again.

Also keep in mind that sugar eaten with a meal retards digestion by inhibiting enzyme action. With digestion halted, the nutrients in the meal are not properly absorbed and can become toxic. Undigested particles of food may be absorbed through the lining of the stomach and the intestinal walls. They then migrate to other parts of the body where they are attacked by the immune system as foreign invaders. These complexes then accumulate in different areas and can cause inflammation that might result in such things as joint pain. These immune complexes may even migrate to the brain where inflammation of tissue can cause headaches or memory problems. See Nancy Appleton's *Lick the Sugar Habit.*

The easiest way to get started or to cut down on sugar again, after you've slipped a bit, is by marking your calendar with sugar-free days. How many days in a row are you managing to go completely without sugar? This helps give strength in those moments of weakness.

The worst thing you can do is eat sugary products by themselves. I used to do this in order to conserve calories. The combination of sugar and/or a starch without substantial protein will lead to an increase in negative side effects. C. Keith Conners, a member of the Department of Psychiatry at Duke University Medical Center in Durham, N.C., discovered in controlled studies that children who ate sugar alone, outside of a balanced meal, tended toward more deviant, destructive behavior and increased hyperactivity. These results include not only mentally disturbed children, but normal children as well. In other studies, levels of aggression could be directly correlated with the ratio of sugar products to nutritional foods consumed.

Keep a journal of your eating habits. Note when you have cravings and if you are eating carbohydrates alone. Record your feelings, thoughts, and symptoms. You might even want to record your weight, measurements, and snap a "before" picture. Do not be too eager for weight loss results. Although heavier people may lose more weight initially, one and one half pound per month is considered healthy weight loss. Do not check your weight too frequently. Daily or even weekly may be too much. Rather, prescribe to the optimal outcome plan: weigh only when you *feel* thinner—no more than once a month. This may take a little self-restraint but it is well worth the effort.

Use discretion in the beginning with whom you share your goals. Sometimes those around us are intimidated by our zealous nature and may even try to thwart our progress. Remember, it is okay for you to put your health (and your appearance) high on your priority list. But long before you see any changes in your physical appearance, your self-esteem will begin to grow as you start to discover the magnitude of good nutrition in your life.

Depression

Over seven billion dollars is spent on antidepressants every year. And nearly one-quarter of all adults experience some kind of mental health crisis annually. Sugar *can* be the cause of depression. According to psychologist Larry Christensen, Ph.D., of the University of Southern Alabama, sugar may trigger a temporary release of pleasure-producing chemicals called endorphins. However, immediately following a sugar binge, endorphins drop to lower than ever levels and "sugar blues" becomes a reality.

The good news is that once sugar is removed from the diet depression may vanish completely. My own experience can attest to this. But keep in mind that for some people it may take up to three weeks before you notice an improvement in mood.

On a virtually sugar free diet I rarely get depressed. In fact, most days I wake up with a smile on my face. A few years ago that was difficult to imagine. My life today is rich with small joys and peace of mind—until I have a sugar lapse. Then I feel the difference. I begin to find fault with everyone and every thing, including myself—especially myself! My life appears bleak, hopeless, and ugly. My husband and I call these episodes the "I hate my life" syndrome. Whenever we feel this way we have learned to ask ourselves this question: Have I had sugar or alcohol in the last three days? The answer is, inevitably, a resounding "Yes!" However, if we can manage to make it through the requisite three-day cleanse (no sugar), the sunshine returns. It is a great blessing to have discovered this key to happiness and contentment. This book is dedicated to the hope that you may unlock this door as well.

Brain Power

Another expression we've developed is "the sugar dumbs." Once, after a very serious birthday binge, my husband (the college graduate) asked me, "How do you spell *when?*"

We began making a connection between sugar consumption and recall memory. At the height of my illness I could not remember my own phone number and once even stood baffled on my doorstep trying to figure out how to insert a key into a lock. My synapses were out of whack.

Have you ever forgotten what you were saying mid-sentence? I used to think that this was just a normal occurrence for everyone—not so! This does not ever happen to us when we are sugar free. Without sugar our minds are alert and fresh (and we don't need caffeine to accomplish this!) I am articulate and my short-term memory is remarkable. No more misplaced keys or forgotten calls and appointments. Want a house and mind free of clutter? Want to shine with efficiency? Then quit sugar!

Problems with cognitive function are a direct result of insufficient fuel to the nervous system. Detecting a high blood sugar level, the pancreas secretes insulin to lower the blood sugar (ironically, in an attempt to save the brain). But, soon the adrenal gland sends cortisol into the blood to help raise the blood sugar again. Cortisol contributes to hyperactivity and actually causes damage to the hippocampus–the memory center! The only way to feel good again (or so we think) is to reach for more sugar. This, of course, starts the vicious cycle all over again. Within 15-20 minutes of a drop in blood sugar symptoms may occur. These can be sudden and severe and may include physical, mental, and emotional disturbances as well as short-term memory problems.

Crime and Road Rage

Half of all women killed in this country are murdered by their spouse or live-in boyfriend. Children are shooting their teachers and each other. "Road Rage" is a household expression. Even air flight crews are being schooled to deal with *air rage.*

No one is immune from this manic scourge. While on vacation last year in the Southwest, I bumped into a disgruntled teenager as he was exiting the library in which my husband was busy at a computer terminal. I noticed that he was cradling something in his arms and when I turned to look back at him I saw that there was an extra cartridge in his back pocket. Fortunately, he had changed his mind about using his AK-47 Assault Rifle on the unsuspecting patrons. Still, it caused quite a stir. He was arrested within a few yards of me and I was questioned as a witness.

For days afterwards I was in shock. This was a small town. Doesn't this kind of thing happen to *other* people? Certainly it could never happen to me; all cliché responses. But the question remained: why this epidemic? Could poor diet actually be a part of this problem? Never in the history of the world has so much sugar been consumed. Is there a connection between sugar and violence?

In *Hypoglycemia: A Better Approach*, Dr. Paavo Airola writes that the heavily sugar-laden American diet has resulted in an epidemic of hypoglycemia. Over twenty million Americans are affected. Because many of the symptoms of this disease are psychological (emotional instability, anxiety, depression, neurosis, and even psychotic episodes), the social implications are enormous. Dr. Airola quotes J. I. Rodale saying that "many accidents, family quarrels, suicides, and even crimes" are committed when an individual's blood sugar levels are pathologically low. The repercussions of a high sugar diet on our personal mental health and on the state of our society are immense. We must begin to take this issue much more seriously.

In an article titled *Hypoglycemia and Driving* Terri D'Arrigo states that ". . . studies have shown that driving performance deteriorates significantly when blood glucose drops below 65mg . . . Below that level you are more likely to swerve, spin, or go off the road." She also writes that symptoms, not only include shakiness and lightheadedness, but irritability, confusion, and anger. Since it is possible to have low blood sugar without overt symptoms, diabetics should test blood glucose prior to driving and hypoglycemics should eat *by the clock.*

Man and womankind were given the desire for sweetness to help them detect edible foods in nature; not to overeat mass marketed sugary foods. We truly are a nation (a world!) of sugar addicts. Remember, you don't have to be hypoglycemic to experience symptoms from a sugar binge. Anyone is prone to the "sugar blues" or the "sugar crazies." The biological explanation for the mood swings and the violent reactive behavior associated with sugar consumption is exactly the same as it is for excess alcohol consumption: a radical metabolic shift due to extreme and subsequent inadequate blood glucose level. On many occasions this is a perceived drop in blood glucose level due to prolonged and extended cellular saturation of excess sugar.

Eating too sweet can also result in the "mean" episode. Everyone has heard of the "mean drunk" but did you know that excess sugar ingestion can also result in violent outbursts? (See Chapter 3: Hypoglycemia/The Food Cure.) It is important to begin to develop this understanding. In the same way that we now understand alcoholism to be a disease so should we recognize sugar addiction and its resultant symptoms. This will help to enlighten those burdened with these symptoms and possibly relieve some of the stigma attached to this kind of behavior.

In the book *Unlimited Power: The Way to Peak Personal Achievement*, Anthony Robbins references the poor diet of a chronic juvenile delinquent (as recounted by Alexander Schauss in his work *Diet, Crime, & Delinquency*). For breakfast this youth ate five bowls of sugar sweetened cereal. Throughout the day he snacked on candy. For lunch he ate a high fat meal of burgers and fries with white bread and dessert. His drinks were sugar sweetened and his dinner consisted of white carbohydrates and dessert. In addition, this child stated that he *added* sugar to almost everything.

Nearly twenty percent of our school age children are now diagnosed with A.D.D. For myself, a teaspoon of sugar a day is enough to trigger symptomatic behavior. The average American consumes nearly two cups a day; up to 140 lbs. a year! Certainly teenagers are at the high end of this spectrum. This boy's symptoms included insomnia, nightmares, headaches, itching and crawling sensations, stomach upset, dizziness, weakness, memory problems, depression, constant worry, emotional outbursts, and short temper. Is it any wonder that we have violent and unstable youth? Studies have proven that poor diet, especially ones high in sugar, *can* result in criminal behavior (See Chapter 1: Sugar is a Drug/Reduce Slowly).

There is no better treatise on the nutritional needs of our children than the book *The Crazy Makers: How the Food Industry is Destroying Our Brains and Harming Our Children*, by Carol Simontacchi. Please read this book. Help save our children. Help save our world.

Not So Sweet on the Environment

The effects of sugar production on our environment are devastating. In the last twenty-five years or so, Florida land planted in sugar cane has doubled to over 400,000 acres. This immense rise in the production of sugar in the Everglades has had a drastic effect on the surrounding ecosystem.

Phosphorus, a by-product of sugar-cane production, stimulates the growth of hemp vine and cattails. These plants inhibit saw grass and other vegetation which are necessary for wildlife to flourish. It also reduces oxygen in the water creating a toxic environment for fish.

Affected wildlife includes turtles, ducks, snakes, herons, and other exotic birds. The numbers of some species have declined radically. Over the last century 90 percent of the wading bird population has been lost. In 1994 an environmental cleanup project was initiated, with sugar companies only footing 15 percent of the bill; the first phase estimated at nearly two-billion dollars. Taxpayers, of course, have been responsible for the rest. In addition, since 1993 Americans have been paying more than a billion dollars a year in higher sugar prices because of strict import quotas created by congress. Domestic sugar beet and sugar cane growers also have access to federally guaranteed loans. *The Wall Street Journal* reported that in 1998 The Federal Sugar Plan cost taxpayers a whopping 1.9 billion dollars.

A sweet deal? You bet. When representatives of the sugar industry try to convince us that sugar consumption is down due to this new anti-sugar *craze* we must consider the source. The truth is that refined sugar intake is up by thirty percent since 1983 with 1999 topping out as the highest sugar consumption year in American history.

How to Find Sugar on the Label

Be sure to check all the processed food you buy. Refined sugar can be contained in some unlikely places. For instance: diet drinks, protein bars, ketchup, soups, pizza, and even bread. Refined sugar may appear on a label as Sugar, Sucrose, Glucose, Invert Sugar, Dextrose, Ribose, Maltose, Malto Dextrin, Isomalt, High Fructose Corn Sweetener or Syrup, Rice Syrup, High Maltose Syrup, High Fructose Complex, Corn Syrup, Turbinado (touted as a healthier option but still lethal), Brown Sugar (merely white table sugar with caramel coloring), or Pure Cane Crystals (pure white sugar!). These are all taboo.

One of the best ways to detect refined sugar in a product is to check the sugar content under *Nutrition Facts*. A naturally sweetened product will usually have no more than twelve to sixteen grams. I have found that twelve grams per serving is the maximum I can tolerate as a hypoglycemic. Of course, tolerance will vary. As a general rule-of-thumb, if the product has more than twenty grams of sugar per serving it is highly likely that the item is loaded with hidden refined sugar. Check every label, keeping a close eye on your symptoms, mood, or behavior following consumption and you will soon become conscious of the differences. Be a sugar detective. Scout it out in order to take control of your life. Also, be conscious of your *overall* carbohydrate count as all carbohydrates eventually convert to glucose in the bloodstream.

My husband, who is not hypoglycemic, has also learned to appreciate the sugar-free lifestyle. He has been relieved of a long-standing condition: Restless Leg Syndrome (RLS) and the elimination of caffeine has resulted in relief from psoriasis as well. Plus, we argue less, have more energy, sleep better, and are less moody when we are sugar free.

Again, here are those numbers repeated:

Three to seven grams per serving is the *maximum* level desired for refined sugar sweetened products (The Sugar Busters! gang suggests only one to three grams). If you are having symptoms of any kind, limit products with refined sugars to three grams of sugar per serving or less. Note: A product does not have to taste sweet to have this much added sugar and even small amounts of real sugar may cause symptoms and/or addiction. Check the label for added sugars.

Zero to twelve grams of natural sugar are great, but hypoglycemics should be wary of using low carbohydrate bars as meal replacements as they may not deliver enough carbohydrates to maintain glucose balance between meals.

Thirteen to twenty grams of sugar per serving is okay for naturally sweetened products but not for refined sugar sweetened products. Twelve grams or above per serving of any sugar, however, may cause symptoms in hypoglycemics. If you are having any symptoms at all limit naturally sweetened products to no more than 12 grams of sugar per serving. Naturally sweetened products will be better tolerated than refined sugar items because of the slower rate of absorption into the blood stream.

Over twenty grams of sugar in a product usually means that it has refined sugar and should be avoided. But even natural food products can be a problem. Consider fruit juice which may have the sugar content of up to eight pieces of fruit in a single glass. Juice is highly condensed and should be avoided by hypoglycemics.

Maximum sugar intake:
Naturally sweetened – 12 grams of sugar per serving
Refined sugars – 3 grams of sugar per serving

Note: Your results may vary. Every individual's specific response to food and nutritional requirements are unique. Age, health, genetic predisposition, emotional wellbeing, and environmental factors must all be considered. These numbers, which are based on the author's personal medical history, are to be used as a guideline only. See your physician to determine your own individual tolerances.

Turbinado. Be on the lookout for Turbinado. It is sold as a healthier white sugar replacement. But it is still sugar. It is, in fact, refined white sugar mixed with a little molasses. I have encountered severe symptoms from it. Often, it will be on a label without any explanation that it is a sugar at all. When you find this, notify the manager of the store that for individuals with dietary restrictions (especially for medical reasons), it is imperative that it be labeled a sugar. Most health food stores label their own baked goods.

Brown Sugar. Shame on everybody for letting us think that Brown Sugar is healthier than White Sugar. Brown Sugar is merely white sugar mixed with caramel coloring. Avoid it!

Pure Cane Crystals. The sugar industry would have us believe that because it is labeled and billed as "pure" that refined white sugar is good for you. Some advertisements go so far as to say that it is "All-natural." Beware of this kind of propaganda. Heroin and marijuana are also "natural" substances.

"Raw" Sugar. Raw sugar is table sugar with beet pulp or cane fiber added to mimic the taste of true raw sugar. Genuine raw sugar is impure and cannot be sold commercially.

Sugar Substitutes

There are many sugar substitutes on the market; some natural, some synthetic. They affect the metabolism in different ways. Some are healthy with little or no side effects; others have severe side effects.

We all know that some of the artificial sweeteners (the ones that come in little packets) have been touted as having potentially harmful side effects. Actually, the jury is still out on that one.

I love the little pink packets. But for the sake of health I began reducing the amount that I used. I once used more than a single packet per cup of coffee. By gradually reducing the amount I added to my cup, I have lowered my *sweet meter* to the point where I only need a pinch out of a packet to satisfy me. The coffee tastes just as sweet to me as it used to and I have reduced the amount of potentially harmful chemicals in my diet. Which, in turn, eases my conscience; something that also affects one's health.

Artificial Sweeteners

Saccharin. Saccharin was removed off the list of likely known carcinogens in May of 2000 by a panel of government toxicologists. Years of research had proven that saccharin does not cause tumor growth in humans.

The chemical was initially listed in 1981 as potentially harmful because it caused tumor growth in rodents. But the amounts of saccharin forced upon the rodents was equal in human consumption to about 600 soft drinks a day; more than any human being would consume in a lifetime.

SWEET 'N LOW® BRAND Granulated Sugar Substitute (Pink Packets)
A blend of nutritive and non-nutritive sweeteners. Ingredients: Nutritive Dextrose, 3.6% Calcium Saccharin (36 mg per packet,) Cream of Tartar, Calcium Silicate (an anti-caking agent). Net Wt. .035 oz (1g), Serving Size 1 packet, Calories 0, Total Fat 0g, Sodium 0mg., Total Carbohydrate less than 1g, Protein 0g. One packet contains the sweetness of 2 teaspoons of sugar. CUMBERLAND PACKING CORP.

SWEET PORTION™ PINK Low Calorie Sugar Substitute (Pink Packets)
Made with nutritive and non-nutritive sweeteners. Ingredients: Dextrose, Calcium Saccharin (40 mg Saccharin), Cream of Tartar, and Calcium Silicate (anti-caking agent). Net Wt. .035 oz. (1g), Serving Size 1 packet, Calories 0, Total Fat 0g, Sodium 0mg, Total Carbohydrate 1g, **Sugars 1g,** Protein 0g. One packet contains the sweetness of 2 teaspoons of sugar. PORTION PAC, INC.

Aspartame. Aspartame is considered the bad boy of sweeteners. Despite U.S. Food and Drug Administration (FDA) approval consumption of aspartame is never safe according to Nexus Magazine.[1] Aspartame may cause cellular damage. Studies have linked aspartame to mammary, ovarian, uterine, and brain tumors. There are also reports that aspartame may be linked to mental retardation, comas, and birth defects.

Aspartame is the technical name for the brand names Nutra Sweet, Equal, Spoonful, and Equal Measure. According to the FDA, some chronic illnesses can be worsened by ingesting aspartame. If you have any of the following disease conditions you should avoid aspartame: multiple sclerosis, epilepsy, chronic fatigue syndrome, parkinson's disease, alzheimer's, lymphoma, fibromyalgia, and diabetes. Since aspartame may block glucose entry to the brain it may exacerbate symptoms of hypoglycemia as well. Infants, children, pregnant women, and the elderly should not have aspartame. If you experience any symptoms whatsoever with the use of aspartame you should discontinue use immediately.

In the studies cited there is no indication that the subjects were sugar free. This is a factor that may have had some weight in the results. Some subjects reported severe symptoms with six to eight servings per day of products containing aspartame. I do not avoid aspartame altogether but I do limit my consumption. The only symptom I have experienced is insomnia with two to three aspartame products a day. This accounts for only seven days in an eight-year period. It is important to note that after I quit sugar and began to have *more* artificially sweetened products my disease symptoms disappeared altogether, except for this one episode. Please, do your own research and make an informed decision for yourself. Access a wide variety of sources. It is never wise to rely upon just one, and that includes diet books! I urge you to read as many books as you can to find the diet that is right for you and educate yourself about nutrition. If you experience any side effects after consuming aspartame or any other artificial sweetener, avoid it. But do keep in mind that sugar may be even more harmful.

According to *The Magazine of Health, Prevention, and Environmental News,*[2] the FDA and the Centres for Disease Control received nearly 7,000 complaints about aspartame between 1981 and 1994, which included five deaths. But when you stop to consider the number of deaths from heart disease, cancer, diabetes, and obesity (all conditions linked to sugar consumption) during that same period, the implications are staggering. Where is the public outcry against sugar? Of course, natural foods are always a better choice than products with artificial ingredients. However, for some, such as diabetics and hypoglycemics who must limit *all* sugars, artificially sweetened products are a wonderful gift. Without them we would not be able to enjoy the same foods as the rest of society.

I have tried to include the *All-natural* alternatives whenever possible. They are noted as such. But this directory is in no way totally inclusive. Still, I have listed most of the foods I have enjoyed; the naturally sweetened lower glycemic options (that do contain some sugar) and the artificially sweetened (safe for diabetics) products that may contain aspartame. It is my hope that in the future, the American food industry will not only allow but encourage the use of more natural and healthier low glycemic sweeteners such as herbal stevia.

Note: The products in this book are how I managed to survive my predisposition to eating sweets (chips and cola!). I found, not necessarily the best choices for health, but the better alternatives to eating the more harmful foods I would have otherwise had anyway. Hello, my name is Sabina, and I am a sugar addict. The original sugar addict. This diet may not be perfect but it is delicious and fun. If you like, you can call it a *transitional* diet; a stepping-stone toward your *perfect diet* (the one that does not include any artificial sweeteners). I just call it survival.

EQUAL SWEETENER® (Blue Packets).
Equal is a registered trademark of The NutraSweet Company.
0 Calories. No Sodium or Saccharin. Sweet as 2 tsp. Sugar. Ingredients: Dextrose with Maltodextrin, **Aspartame**. Net Wt. 0.035 oz. (1 gram) One packet contains less than 1 gram of carbohydrates. Phenylketonurics: Contains Phenylalanine.

Many of the products listed in this book do contain aspartame, or phenyl-alanine, an ingredient that should be avoided by persons with phenylketo-nuria (PKU). Please read your labels carefully and do your own research to help you make an informed decision for yourself regarding these products and their ingredients. To avoid risk of health, see a physician prior to starting this or any other diet.

Acesulfame K (Sunette). This artificial sweetener was approved by the FDA in 1988. It is calorie-free and about two-hundred times as sweet as white sugar. It is frequently added to commercial food products and has been proven safe in more than ninety different studies.

Sucralose (Splenda) was approved in 1998. This sweetener, derived from sugar, is nearly six-hundred times as sweet. However, it is indigestible so it has zero calories and is also added frequently to food.

Polyols. Some of the products listed contain the artificial sweeteners Maltitol, Sorbitol, and Lactitol. Sorbitol (d-Glucitol) is rice based. These sweeteners are referred to as "Sugar Alcohols" and are non-carcinogenic, compatible for diabetics, and lower in calories than regular sugar (sucrose). The FDA requires that this term (Sugar Alcohols) be used in the Nutrition Facts panel to list this group of artificial sweeteners. Some of the products listed contain these "Sugar Alcohols" that include Isomalt. These sweeteners do not contain sugar or alcohol.

Warning: Although these products are delicious, they should be eaten sparingly. If consumed in excess they may have some unpleasant side effects. There is usually a warning on the label specifying "laxative effect." The inability of the gastrointestinal tract to absorb these processed sweeteners quickly may result in some abdominal discomfort. There is no reason why these delicious treats, however, cannot be part of a healthy diet.

Jane, of Diabeatit.com (Dia-beat-it) comments that paying attention to the serving size is key. Don't over-do-it with artificial sweeteners. She loves Maltitol sweetened Bridge Mix but noticed effects when she nibbled indiscriminately. "Of course," she says, "when I over ate regular sugar I would get a headache the size of Texas! And when I think about how refined sugar affects my health it should carry an even bigger warning on all of the packages that contain it!"

Do not be tempted to revert back to refined sugar if you have a negative experience with the "tols." Although the ill effects from these products may appear harmful, it is much more important to maintain glucose balance for longevity and disease prevention. Glucose balance is the key to good health and weight control.

A friend once commented, "Moderation in all things . . . even moderation." I think those moments of excess are there to remind us just how important moderation is.

Natural Sweeteners

In your local health food store you can find many natural sugar substitutes. Look on the label for **Brown Rice Syrup, Barley Malt sweetened, Fruit Juice sweetened, Cane Juice, Fruit sweetened, Fructose, and naturally occurring Lactose** in dairy products. These are all sweetening substances that metabolize more slowly than refined sugar.

Natural sweeteners, since they are not over-processed to begin with, metabolize at a slower rate of absorption in your system. Because of this, they do not produce many of the negative side effects of refined sugar (unless, of course, you eat a pound of cane juice sweetened chocolate at one sitting!) It is important to remember that ultimately, sugar is still sugar. With sufficient quantities (of even natural sugars) you may still experience some negative side effects. Below are listed some natural (less processed) sugar options along with a few brand name resources.

Barley Malt. Barley Malt is kind of a beer-flavored honey. The process of sprouting Barley Malt turns starch to sugars. In recipes, Barley Malt Syrup replaces Honey and Molasses one to one. To replace sugar, use 1/4 cup less liquid for each cup of Barley Malt used.

EDEN® Organic Barley Malt Traditional Malt Syrup.
Certified organically grown and made, traditionally malted pure barley syrup . . . . *A More Intelligent Sweetener.*
Net Wt. 20 oz. (1 lb. 4 oz) 560g, Serving Size 1 Tbsp. (21g), Servings 27, Calories 60, Fat Calories 0, Total Fat 0g, Saturated 0g, Cholesterol 0mg, Sodium 0mg, Potassium 65mg, Total Carbohydrate 14g, **Sugars 8g**, Protein 1g. Ingredients: Organic Sprouted Barley. EDEN FOODS, INC.

Brown Rice Syrup. Rice-based sweeteners are commonly believed to be very low in allergy causing agents and are especially suited for consumers with allergies to corn based sweeteners. Rice is also high in antioxidants and Vitamin E, ingredients recognized for their anti-aging properties.

SWEET CLOUD® Organic Brown Rice Malt Syrup Sweetener.
. . . *traditionally crafted using only naturally occurring enzymes from organic malted whole barley.* Available at your health foods market.

Net Wt 16 oz. (454g), Serving Size 1 Tbsp. (20g), Servings 22, Calories 65, Fat Calories 0, Total Fat 0g, Saturated Fat 0g, Cholesterol 0mg, Sodium 0mg, Total Carbohydrate 16g, **Sugars 16g**, Protein 1g. Ingredients: Organic Brown Rice, Organic Malted Barley, Water. GREAT EASTERN SUN, Made in Belgium.

TREE OF LIFE® Rice Syrup Brown Rice Sweetener.
Net Wt. 11 oz. (325 ml), Serving Size 2 Tbsp., Servings 11, Calories 120, Fat Calories 5, Total Fat 1/2 g, Sodium 5mg, Total Carbohydrate 29g, Vitamin A 2%. Ingredients: Selected Whole Brown Rice, Organic Sprouted Barley Grain, and Water. TREE OF LIFE, INC.

Dehydrated Cane Juice. Dehydrated cane juice is less processed than refined sugar. It is mechanically harvested after the cane has been pressed, leaving many of the natural ingredients intact. Dehydrated Cane Juice has as many as ten less processing steps than refined white sugar.

ESCULENT™ Dehydrated Cane Juice.
Available at natural foods markets. Net Wt. 16 oz. (1 lb) 454g, Serving Size 1 tsp. (4g), Sugars 113, Calories 16, Fat Calories 0, Total Fat 0g, Sodium 0mg, Total Carbohydrate 4g, **Sugars 4g.** AMERICAN NATURAL SNACKS.

WHOLESOME™ FOODS Organic Sugar Evaporated Cane Juice.
No Herbicides. No Pesticides. 100% Certified Organic Sugar Cane.
Found in natural foods stores. Net Wt. 1 lb. (16 oz.) 453g, Serving Size 1 tsp. (4g), Servings 100, Calories 16, Fat Calories 0, Total Fat 0g, Sodium 0mg, Potassium 0mg, Total Carbohydrate 4g, **Sugars 4g.**

Fructose. Fructose is not to be confused with High Fructose Corn Syrup (a high glycemic food additive that should be avoided). Fructose is simply condensed fruit sugar. Among the three primary sugars (glucose from starches, galactose from dairy, and fructose from fruit) fructose is the slowest processing. However, although fructose metabolizes more slowly than sucrose (white table sugar), large amounts of fructose should be avoided. In large doses, fructose can increase your total cholesterol level, including the "bad" cholesterol (LDL).

Hypoglycemics and diabetics should also note that fruit and fruit juice are extremely high in sugar, albeit natural. A glass of fruit juice (and it need not be "sugar added") can have as much sugar as that in eight pieces of whole fruit—without the benefit of dietary fiber—up to forty grams of sugar per serving! Please avoid fruit juice.

As a hypoglycemic, I must limit my fruit intake to less than one serving a day. This is unfortunate as I used to love to eat fruit. But more than one serving a day, now results in symptoms that include anxiety, insomnia, chills, and dark negative thoughts. Fructose-sweetened products give me no problems unless I over indulge.

SWEET LITE® Natural Fructose Sugar.
The Dieter's Sugar . . . avoid the problems of common sugar! All Natural. No Aftertaste. For sweetening, baking, and cooking. 50 Individual Packets. Also available in liquid and bulk 8 oz. pouch. Net Wt. 5 oz. (142g), Serving size 1 packet (2.83g), Servings per container 50, Calories 10, Total Fat 0g, Sodium 0mg, Total Carbohydrate 3g, **Sugars 3g**, Protein 0g. Crystalline fructose.
Note to Diabetics: This product may be useful in your diet on the advice of a physician. This is not a reduced calorie food. Fructose is a carbohydrate which must be accounted for in the diet. Fructose cannot be used to counteract an insulin reaction. One teaspoon of SweetLite® Fructose is approximately 1/3 fruit exchange. TKI Foods, Inc. (For fructose sweetened recipes see Resource Section at the back of this book.)

Honey. Honey is the only nonacid-forming sweetener. However, one tablespoon of honey is equivalent to three teaspoons of regular sugar, and it should be avoided by both diabetics and hypoglycemics. For others, honey may be taken as an alternative sweetener to refined sugar, but only in limited amounts, as honey's sweetness is chiefly derived from sucrose.

Sucrose is absorbed too quickly into the bloodstream causing the body to react by discharging insulin. In order to efficiently break down and absorb proteins and fats, the small amount of carbohydrate needed by our digestive system can easily be obtained by taking nonrefined carbohydrates such as whole grains and vegetables.

Stevia. Stevia is derived from a South American shrub. Originally used by the Paraguayan Indians, stevia was later discovered by the South American scientist, Antonio Bertoni in 1887. The glycosides in stevia are extremely sweet, up to three hundred times sweeter than table sugar, and the main ingredient, stevioside, is virtually calorie free. The leaf itself and a whole leaf concentrate are a nutritious dietary supplement that is only about 30 times as sweet as sugar and has many health benefits.

Scientific research has shown stevia to effectively regulate blood sugar levels. It also tends to lower elevated blood pressure without seeming to affect normal blood pressure. It inhibits the growth of some bacteria and infectious organisms, including the bacteria that cause tooth decay and gum disease. It may even reduce the incidence of colds and flu, especially when used as a mouthwash or added to toothpaste.

Initial research indicates that stevia may work as an aid to weight loss by suppressing the appetite mechanism. In addition, it may reduce a craving for sweets and high fat foods with some people claiming a reduction in their desire for tobacco and alcoholic beverages as well. Stevia improves digestion and gastrointestinal function, soothes an upset stomach, and reportedly boosts the immune system.

According to Healthfree.com there has never been a complaint of any harmful side effects from stevia in nearly 1500 years of use. Dr. Daniel Mowrey states, "Few substances have ever yielded such consistently negative results in toxicity trials as have stevia . . . No abnormalities in weight change, food intake, cell or membrane characteristics, enzyme and substrate utilization, or chromosome characteristics. No cancer, birth defects, no acute and no chronic untoward effects. Nothing."

The leaf contains proteins, fibers, carbohydrates, iron, phosphorus, calcium, potassium, sodium, magnesium, zinc, rutin (a flavonoid), Vitamin A, Vitamin C, and an oil that contains fifty-three other constituents (See www.healthfree.com). South American natives have been utilizing stevia as a sweetener for centuries and today it is the main sweetening agent in soft drink manufacturing south of the border. The Japanese have used it since the 1970s, consuming about ninety percent of the world's stevia leaf supply. It is available in the United States but only as a supplement.

Stevia, to be used as a more desirable sweetener, can be found in either a powder or a liquid at your local health food store. It works well in baked goods as it is heat stable and has a low glycemic index. This is good news for diabetics, as it does not cause a shift in the glucose level. The whole leaf or whole leaf concentrate are a better choice for nutritional health benefits. Check the Internet for more information, recipes, and applications. Some sites are listed under the Resources section of this book.

NOW® FOODS Stevia Extract.
Natural Herb, Calorie Free, Saccharin Free, Aspartame Free. Contains no soy, yeast, wheat, milk, synthetics, artificial colors, flavors, or preservatives. 100 Packet Box, Net Wt. 3.5 oz. (100g), Serving Size 1 Packet, Calories 0, Fat Calories 0, Sodium 0mg, Total Carbohydrate 1g, **Sugars 1g**. NOW FOODS, INC.

SWEET & BETTER, *A Super Stevia™product.*
Sugar free, all natural, calorie free, safe for diabetics.
1 oz. Liquid Concentrate BODY ECOLOGY. Call 1-800-4-Stevia for more information.

Lo Han Fruit Extract. HerbaSway® is derived from the Lo Han Fruit, which is found in China. There are no artificial ingredients and it has zero calories per serving. It is also low glycemic and there are even claims that it helps burn fat stores. It is only available in liquid form with seven drops equivalent to about a teaspoon of sugar. It too may be used hot or cold and is available at health food stores.

Xylitol. The Ultimate Sweetener® is derived from birch sugar, sometimes referred to as xylitol. It is a sugar alcohol that is absorbed into the gastrointestinal tract at a very slow rate. This slow rate of absorption places it low on the glycemic index. It does not cause tooth decay and is often found in sugarless chewing gum. In baking, one cup of The Ultimate Sweetener equals one cup of refined sugar. Not found in stores, this product can only be acquired by contacting the company Ultimate Life at their website www.ultimatelife.com.

---

[1] Nexus Magazine, Volume 2, #2 (Oct-Nov 1995), Volume 3, #1 (Dec 1995, Jan 1996), P.O. Box 30, Mapleton, QLD 4560, Australia.

[2]Mullarkey, Barbara Alexander and Adell V. Newman, *Sweet Delusion–How Safe is Your Artificial Sweetener?, Part One: The Hidden History of Aspartame,* The Magazine of Health, Prevention, and Environmental News, May/June 1994, Vol. 1, Issue 4.

Chapter 2
Diabetes

The nurse that was not "scrubbed in", as I was, came around to our side of the operating room table. She reached inside the doctor's surgical gown and loosened the string on his blue scrub pants. They fell silently to the floor. The blood from the amputation had soaked them so severely that he could not leave the room without changing.

I handed the limb to the outside nurse. After so many years the weight of a man's leg still astounded me. The anesthesiologist adjusted a valve on his I.V. and I looked at our patient. He was no longer a complete person. The staff accepted this procedure as routine. But would he? He was a diabetic who had neglected to check his feet for minor injuries.

Over my ten-year period as a surgical nurse this incident repeated itself time and time again. How can we measure the psychological impact of such an event? The potential biological and subsequent psychological damage of high blood sugar levels are immeasurable. Some of these problems include blood vessel and nerve damage, sexual dysfunction, and loss of sensation leading to infections from minor injuries that could result in ultimate amputation of extremities. Contrary to popular culture, sugar consumption is a pastime that should not be taken lightly.

Think diabetes is something that only happens to a few? Fifty per-cent of America's population can now be considered "pre-diabetic." That means that the insulin producing capacity of these people (odds are 50/50 that you are one) is barely enough to handle their daily "sugar load."

In the last twenty years there have been more deaths from diabetes than all the deaths from the world's wars in the last one hundred years. And so many children are now developing Type-2 Diabetes, that the term *adult-onset diabetes* is becoming obsolete. According to an article in *Newsweek* magazine, diabetes is being hailed as "the next great lifestyle disease epidemic."[3] Diagnosed cases increased by a third between 1990 and 1998 with a seventy percent increase among people in their thirties. It is no longer a disease of the aging. These are disturbing statistics. The word *lifestyle*, however, infers that there is something that we can do to change it.

Sugar molecules in the bloodstream are the primary source of energy for muscle and nerve cells. With diabetes the body can no longer metabolize these molecules. Blood glucose rises up to three times the normal level taxing the kidneys as they try to eliminate the excess glucose from the blood stream.

The American Diabetes Association stresses that over time, high blood sugar levels can damage both blood vessels and nerves. This may result in inadequate blood flow to the hands and feet as well as the legs, arms, and especially the vital organs. Poor blood flow to these areas increases one's risk of infections, heart problems, stroke, blindness, and kidney disease. Diabetic men have double the risk of heart disease and women have four times the normal rate.

With blood vessel and nerve damage to the extremities you might either lose feeling in your feet or have increased pain in your feet and legs. Without sensation you would be vulnerable to even the most minor injury which could lead to serious infection and ultimately, amputation.

Damage to blood vessels and nerves may also lead to sexual dysfunction; problems that are difficult to treat and may require surgery, often an unattractive, ablative option. For all these reasons, life with sugar is not merely "a piece of cake" as the sugar industry would have you believe but rather a game of Russian Roulette. Which healthy function will be the first to go?

The good news is that many diabetics may treat their condition through diet alone. The ADA states that Type-2 diabetics who have been on medication for their diabetes may be able to go off this medication with a program of proper exercise and diet if some insulin production still exists.

Diabetics may also suffer from clinical hypoglycemia. Since insulin and sugar level must be balanced with each other, if a diabetic gives himself too much insulin he may develop a condition referred to as hyperinsulinism, which ultimately results in a severe drop in blood sugar level or hypoglycemia. Symptoms of hypoglycemia soon follow including anxiety episodes, heart palpitations, lethargy, etc. But, of course, the real culprit of this crisis is the initial high blood sugar level. Three to seven percent of deaths in Type-1 diabetes are due to hypoglycemia complications.

Below you will find a list of high blood sugar symptoms. It is possible to have transient episodes of high blood sugar related directly to heavy sugar consumption. Eating too frequently may also cause a blood sugar imbalance. If you have some of these symptoms it does not necessarily mean that you are diabetic. But do see a doctor immediately if you have any of these symptoms frequently.

SYMPTOMS OF HIGH BLOOD SUGAR:

1. More hungry or thirsty than usual   _____
2. Dry mouth, dry painful eyes   _____
3. More frequent urination   _____
4. Must get up at night to go the bathroom   _____
5. Tired, sleepy, or no energy   _____
6. Sensitivity to light, seeing halos when looking at lights   _____
7. Double vision (due to nerve damage within the eyes)   _____
8. Easily agitated, quick to anger   _____
9. Cold extremities (arms, fingers, toes), chills, hot flashes   _____
10 May have acute sensitivity to sound   _____
11. A buzzing sensation, especially in the midsection   _____
12. Frequent infections   _____
13. Sores that won't heal   _____

If you have checked several of these symptoms and suspect that you may be diabetic, see a physician immediately. Some of the products listed in this book may not be safe for diabetics. Consult your doctor before beginning this or any other diet.

Obesity and Disease

The National Institute of Health states that if you are more than thirty pounds overweight you are technically obese and at risk for weight related medical problems. The obese are at greater risk for high blood pressure, heart disease, diabetes (85% of all diabetics are over weight or technically obese), stroke, gallbladder disease, osteoarthritis, cancer, and respiratory problems including sleep apnea.

According to the *Journal of the American Medical Association* (JAMA, 10/27/99), the problem of obesity in America has reached epidemic proportions. In the 1990s alone, the rate of obesity in America rose by an unbelievable fifty percent! Half the U.S. population now considers themselves overweight and the problem is not only a cosmetic issue. Obesity is lethal. Researchers at the St. Luke's Roosevelt Hospital Center in New York City estimate that approximately 325,000 deaths per year can be attributed to excess body fat.[4] Even children are not immune to its ravaging effects. We are spending almost one hundred billion dollars a year at weight loss treatment centers and health care facilities. Yet, this myopic focus on low-fat eating has done nothing to quell the problem.

In a study of twelve obese teenage boys, Dr. David Ludwig, M.D., director of the obesity program at the Children's Hospital in Boston, examined the different effects of low and high glycemic diets on children. He found that boys who had ingested high glycemic meals (high sugar content) consumed up to eighty-three percent more calories (about 700 additional calories a day!) than the boys who ate low glycemic meals. That easily adds up to an extra twenty pounds of weight gain per year.

Besides being overweight, how do you tell if you are eating high glycemic? If you are hungry only two hours after a meal then you are probably eating the wrong foods. The good news is that reducing sugar, white foods (white breads, white rice, and white pasta), and adding whole grain foods will lengthen the space between your meals. More space equals fewer calories. The results: weight loss and more energy so that you might even *feel* like exercising!

---

[3] Adler, Jerry and Claudia Kalb, *An American Epidemic: Diabetes-The Silent Killer*, Newsweek, September 4, 2000, p. 40-47.

[4] Energy Times, Eating, Exercising, and Weight Control, Part 1, p. 72, October 2000.

Chapter 3
Hypoglycemia:
The Invisible Disease

T here is a common misconception that if you have "low blood sugar" it is reasonable to ingest refined sugar to raise the blood glucose level. Only in an emergency situation should this be considered an alternative. Unbelievably enough, even in the professional medical environment in which I worked as a surgical scrub nurse, no one was aware of the extreme danger of giving a hypoglycemic candy on a regular basis. When I was not able to leave the operating room suite, a nurse would push a piece of hard candy into my mouth behind my mask. Ironically, this and my frequent eating of sugar-loaded energy bars and diet drinks exacerbated my condition to the point where hypoglycemic symptoms eventually led to poor job performance and the loss of my nursing position.

My symptoms included insomnia, frantic pacing, tapping compulsively on my surgical tray, the inability to concentrate, short term memory problems (I could not remember the sequence of my cases from day to day even though I had been doing them for years), afternoon lethargy (which included slurred speech and drowsiness), anxiety attacks, and nightmares.

The Food Cure
Certain foods can exacerbate or diminish the symptoms of hypoglycemia. When we eat carbohydrates or sugar, the level of sugar (glucose) in our blood rises. To compensate for this rise in blood sugar the pancreas releases the hormone insulin. Insulin works to stabilize this rise by bringing the blood sugar level back within normal parameters.

When the blood glucose falls below the critical level the brain, which needs adequate amounts of glucose to function, begins to send out a message requesting more glucose which translates to a carbohydrate or sugar craving. If the brain does not get the glucose it needs, it will start to shut down leaving you feeling light headed, dizzy, or forgetful. You also lose the ability to concentrate.

This state is known as *hypoglycemia* or *low blood sugar*. The expression "low blood sugar" is misleading and has been the cause of much suffering. One naturally assumes that if your blood sugar is low you must eat sugar to bring it back to a normal level. Unfortunately, by doing so you merely begin the vicious cycle all over again.

If you eat a large lunch of white flour items (bread, pasta, pastry) or high glycemic carbohydrates (potatoes, corn, dessert) without a sufficient amount of protein to compensate for the rise in blood sugar, by three o'clock in the afternoon you will be so drowsy that you can hardly keep your eyes open. In extreme cases, like mine, you may even experience slurred speech or blurred vision. If you are not in a position to balance this fall in blood glucose level (perhaps you cannot eat at work) then you may start experiencing other symptoms, such as headaches, nausea, and crankiness later in the day. If you compensate with candy, the cycle begins again except at a more accelerated pace. By evening you will be so "wired" that you cannot sleep or think clearly. Your energy will be sapped from all the ups and downs of your erratic metabolism. Hypoglycemia, unchecked by proper nutrition may develop into more serious conditions such as a thyroid disorder or diabetes.

It is not too difficult, really, to figure out why untreated hypoglycemia may evolve into diabetes. If a gland must continually secrete insulin to counter a high sugar or high starch diet it will eventually be taxed to exhaustion and ultimately malfunction. The pancreas that has been working so hard to produce insulin to bring the blood sugar level down eventually can produce no insulin whatsoever. This then results in consistent high blood sugar or diabetes. Here's the clincher. Whether your problem is low blood sugar or high blood sugar, treatment consists of avoiding sugar. We all know that the diabetic must not eat sugar. Now we know that in order to avoid diabetes the hypoglycemic should not eat sugar. *And* to avoid becoming hypoglycemic *everyone* should avoid sugar!

One of the telltale signs of hypoglycemia is a house in disarray. When the hypoglycemic eats sugar lethargy ensues. Combined with negative symptoms such as migraine headaches, short-term memory problems, and lack of concentration, who can get anything done? Today my house is in order and I actually finish the projects I start. The benefits of good health may be more than you can imagine right now. The book you have always wanted to write, the painting waiting for the artist to awaken . . . these lost dreams may once again be at your fingertips.

Are *you* hypoglycemic? Perhaps you've never been tested. Here is a list of symptoms for you to check. If you suspect that you might be hypoglycemic after checking this list, see a doctor. But remember to educate yourself well and begin by moving toward a sugar-free lifestyle. Read *Hypoglycemia: A Better Approach* by Dr. Paavo Airola or *Hypoglycemia: The Disease Your Doctor Won't Treat* by Jeraldine Saunders and Dr. Harvey M. Ross. Both are great books introducing you to the nutritional approach to disease treatment. These books will also leave you well armed for your doctor visit.

Check this list again, several weeks from now. Note the changes. And, most importantly, do not be intimidated by your physician if his attitude is less than supportive. I once asked a doctor why he never gave his patients nutritional counseling. His response was, "Nobody would follow it anyway." I had seen seventeen different doctors (not uncommon in the military) when I finally announced to my physician that I was taking control of my health through "nutritional therapy." He literally rolled his eyes at me and told me that I had better have surgery before it was too late. It has been eight years since he said that; eight years without drugs, radiation, or surgery (or frequent visits to doctors!). My thyroid is intact and my health is better than ever.

SYMPTOMS OF LOW BLOOD SUGAR:

Feel free to check off this list with symptoms that you are now experiencing. Or photocopy it to help you monitor changes in your physiology as you progress.

1. Anxiety (excessive worry, running train of thoughts) _____
2. Panic attacks (a feeling of impending doom or death) _____
3. Short term memory problems/Forgetting mid-sentence _____
4. Insomnia _____
5. Nightmares/Night terrors _____
6. Irritable (short-tempered, easily agitated, "road rage") _____
7. Frequent arguments _____
8. Trembling or "floppy" weak hands _____
9. Low energy/Lethargic (all you want to do is lie around) _____
10. Heart racing _____
11. Vision problems (blurring, halos, cracks) _____
12. Palpitations (heart flutter) _____
13. Increased heart rate _____
14. Mood swings _____
15. Depression/Crying spells _____

16. Excessive yawning   ——
17. Dark negative thoughts   ——
18. Aching joints   ——
19. Hot flashes   ——
20. Pacing or tapping   ——
21. Chills/Sweats   ——
22. Nausea/Chronic indigestion   ——
23. Nervousness
    (restlessness, excessive shyness, inability to speak)   ——
24. Headaches/Migraines   ——
25. Gums bleeding/Sensitive teeth   ——
26. Paranoia   ——
27. Hallucinations   ——
28. Ringing or Heart pounding in ears   ——
29. Restless Leg Syndrome   ——
30. Muscle ache   ——
31. Suicidal thoughts/Feeling like you are "going crazy"   ——

You may find that some symptoms of low blood sugar and high blood sugar are the same. This is not surprising in that hypoglycemia is actually the adaptive stage of the development of hyperglycemia or high blood sugar.

If not checked, by reducing sugar intake, your pancreas may become exhausted, losing its capacity to regulate blood sugar. This signals the transition from the adaptive (or addictive) stage of disease development to the degenerative stage (diabetes) where the body can no longer rebound to a healthy state. Your symptoms become chronic and complete loss of organ function is inevitable.

Why The Fat Get Fatter

As we have already learned, when you eat a meal or snack high in carbohydrates a rapid rise in blood glucose will occur. The pancreas must then secrete the hormone insulin to adjust for this rise in blood sugar. This insulin is responsible for lowering the blood glucose level. The increased levels of insulin also tell the body not to release fat stores. Our fat then becomes unavailable as ready energy.

Have you ever wondered why the fat seem to get fatter and fatter even though they seem to be eating the same amount of food or even less? The answer to all this is the rate or speed at which carbohydrates enter the blood stream because that is what maintains the rate of insulin secretion. Carbohydrates can be distinguished from one another by this rate.

Simple sugars like fructose and whole grain products enter the blood stream much more slowly than candy, sweet drinks, or "white food" carbohydrates like processed pasta and enriched white bread. The speed at which a carbohydrate enters the blood stream is known as its *glycemic index*. When the glycemic index of a food is low, the absorption rate into the blood is slow. The reason for this is that all "complex" carbohydrates must be broken down into simple sugars for absorption.

The type of sugar obtained from starches (glucose) is the fastest. Fructose, primarily found in fruit, is the slowest. And then we have galactose, found in dairy products. Glucose (sugar) is the only type that can enter the blood stream directly. Fiber is also a contributing factor. The higher the fiber content of a food, the closer it is to its natural state, and the slower its rate of absorption. Since removal of food's fiber increases the rate of absorption juicing is not necessarily a good option.

Glycogen. Glycogen is comprised of glucose molecules that are stored in the liver and the muscles. The glycogen that is stored in the muscles is not accessible to the brain. Only the glycogen stored in the liver can enter the blood stream to maintain adequate blood sugar levels for proper brain function.

However, the glycogen stored in the liver can be depleted within ten to twelve hours. This is why it is absolutely imperative that we do not skip meals or the opposite—overeat. If we overconsume carbohydrates the glycogen levels are filled and the excess carbohydrates have only one alternative: to be converted into fat and stored for all the world to see. We each have our favorite storage site. Some bodies prefer the hips, some the tummy. But wherever your body chooses to store its excess carbohydrates, there will always be room for more.

Insulin. Insulin's primary job is to maintain fat storage. We store fat when there is too much glucose in our system (from eating too many carbohydrates) or too many amino acids from the protein we eat. This excess glucose is easily turned into fat and stored in adipose tissue throughout the body. But insulin can also work to halt that same fat from being burned as energy.

Glucagon. Glucagon, not to be confused with glycogen (too bad they sound so much alike–think "gone" for fat gone!) is the biological opposite of insulin. It is responsible for the release of stored carbohydrates, in the form of glucose from the liver. Once this release is stimulated by glucagon (initiated by protein ingestion), the stored glucose enters the bloodstream, and helps maintain the balance of blood sugar that is necessary for adequate brain function.

Why doesn't the liver supply blood glucose when the body needs it during a state of hypoglycemia? The answer is the high level of insulin in the blood. Remember that insulin is also a blocking agent. Without the proper ratio of protein to carbohydrate the liver is shut down and cannot deliver it's stored glucose.

In summary then, insulin reduces blood sugar levels while glucagon increases blood sugar levels. Keeping carbohydrate intake balanced with protein is the key to weight control. One of the ways to guarantee reduced carbohydrate consumption is to eliminate refined sugar from our diets.

What is the lesson from all this? We should never eat carbohydrates on their own, but always with a balance of protein. The correct ratio is somewhere between one to one or three-quarters protein (in mg) to one of carbohydrate. For example: 15 mg protein for every 20 mg carbohydrate serving. See Dr. Barry Sear's book *The Zone: A Dietary Roadmap* for more extensive information about carbohydrate and protein balancing. Food-combining advocates advise eating only complex carbohydrates (like vegetables) with proteins, no simple (starch) carbohydrates. You can do your own research to find what works best for you.

The best medicine then is to eat several small meals, evenly spaced throughout the day, with the correct ratio of protein to carbohydrate. With a balanced diet of carbohydrates and protein, your calorie consumption will be cut in half because you will be accessing stored fat for energy instead of craving and eating more carbohydrates and sugary treats (an inefficient energy source).

Constant hunger and cravings will be eliminated because your blood-sugar levels will be maintained at a more constant level. You will now be able to go four or five hours between meals without cravings or hunger. When you do finally feel hungry your body is in the process of burning stored fat. Not only will you be losing stored fat between every meal, but your muscular endurance will improve because stored muscle glycogen is being preserved. You will feel less muscle fatigue (a classic hypoglycemic symptom) and have greater endurance.

All you have to remember is no sugar and no carbohydrates by themselves. Balance every meal with both protein and carbohydrates (preferably whole grains or vegetables.) Avoid white foods (white rice, white bread, and white pasta) which have been stripped of their nutritive properties. With the original outer husk removed these products must leach the body's vitamins and minerals in order to be metabolized. They are also higher on the glycemic index.

Summary:

Carbohydrates
1.   Carbohydrates are broken down into glucose.
2.   Glucose affects insulin level in the bloodstream.
3.   Carbohydrates eaten alone or too many carbohydrates (or sugars) equal a higher level of insulin.
4.   A high level of insulin sends a message to hold fat burning and store excess carbohydrates as fat.

Protein
1.   Protein is broken down to amino acids.
2.   Amino acids affect the release of the hormone glucagon from the pancreas which stimulates the burning of fat.
3.   Too much protein or too little carbohydrate equals ketosis (an unhealthy state). Ketone bodies (an abnormal chemical) are eliminated through urination.
4.   This results in a loss of water weight and a strain on the kidneys.

A balance of protein with carbohydrate equals balanced insulin level and stimulation of fat burning.

The Wise Diet
One of the astounding benefits of following a low sugar diet is the increase in physical stamina. I have found that I now have more energy in my forties for my martial arts practice than I had in my teens. As a karate and yoga instructor I have shared my "Diet for Optimum Performance" with my students.

No to Low Refined Sugar except on birthdays and holidays (and then, do try to have it with a well-balanced high-protein meal). Water with lemon or a squirt of iced tea, sugar-free caffeine-free soda pop, sugar-free candy, sugar-free chocolate, or sugar-free ice-cream only. Refined sugar depletes energy and alertness. It also promotes disease conditions.

Water. Minimum two to three sports bottles (24 oz. each) of water every day. If you exercise or are exposed to heat you will need even more. It is better to sip continuously throughout the day rather than just drink with meals as this aids digestion. Consider water being poured over a dry sponge vs. a slow steady drip. Which absorbs more?

Drink purified or spring water rather than distilled. Distilled water, because of the distillation process, is depleted of minerals that are needed for all bodily functions. Generally, most tap water is safe for consumption unless it has a bad taste or smell or is highly chlorinated. It is more important that you never miss an opportunity for hydration rather than wait for a particular type of water.

Water increases energy, boosts the immune system, prevents cramping, and promotes better vision. You simply must read *Your Body's Many Cries for Water: You Are Not Sick, You Are Thirsty* by Fereydoon Batmanghelidj (Global Health Solutions). I have seen a profound improvement in allergies and colds since applying the information in Mr. Batmanghelidj's book.

Meal Spacing. Eat four to five well-balanced small meals, evenly spaced throughout the day. The body needs a complete restoration of nutrition and carbohydrates at least every four hours (hypoglycemics or athletes may need to eat more frequently). A whole grain and sugar-free diet allows you to lengthen the space between meals. This promotes weight loss and increases agility and speed. Glucose balance is maintained.

Meal spacing is the absolute key to weight control. When I was first diagnosed with hypoglycemia I was told to eat every two hours. The result was weight gain but without eliminating the sugar and white foods from my diet, I could not increase this space without becoming symptomatic. After I quit eating refined sugar I noticed that I could go up to four or five hours without symptoms. The weight just fell off.

The Meal Spacing
Weight Loss Formula

STEP 1

Determine how frequently you eat. Begin by keeping a journal of your meals (including snacks!) for one week. Keep track, not only of *what* you eat, but *when* you eat. Write down the *times* that you eat.

STEP 2

Calculate the average space between your meals (including snacks). For instance, if you have breakfast at 8 A.M., a snack at 10 A.M., lunch at noon, dinner at 5 P.M., and a snack at 8 P.M.:

$$
\begin{aligned}
8\text{-}10 &= 2 \text{ hours} \\
10\text{-}12 &= 2 \text{ hours} \\
12\text{-}5 &= 5 \text{ hours} \\
5\text{-}8 &= 3 \text{ hours} \\
\\
\text{Total} &= 12 \text{ hours} \\
\div\ &4 \text{ times eating} \\
\\
&= 3 \text{ hour average}
\end{aligned}
$$

This means that you eat, on average, every 3 hours. The trick then, is to decrease your overall calories by increasing this time span. Be cautious, however. Each meal should be balanced. Do not eat carbohydrates alone. Include protein and fresh vegetables whenever possible. If you decrease your calories without the proper nutrition to compensate, your health could be compromised. Learn to understand your body's nutritional requirements. This is far more important, in the long run, than losing a few pounds quickly.

STEP 3

Adjust your eating times to the next hour. For instance, if your average eating time is 3 hours, move to 4. If it is 4 hours, move to 5. Start counting from the time you end your meal, not from the time you begin eating. But remember, do not ever go past 6 hours. This constitutes skipping a meal, which is detrimental both to your health and to your weight loss plan.

Buy a watch with an alarm that you can set to go off at the next designated mealtime. Be sure to reset it from the end of your meal to the beginning of the next one. For example: I begin eating at noon and end at 12:30. My watch went off at 12:00. Now I reset it for 5:30 P.M. (five hours from the *end* of my meal).

Be aware of your body (as outlined in this book or through your physician's guidance). If you become symptomatic, eat more frequently. Ultimately, the goal is perfectly balanced nutrition as well as a lean (and sexy) body.

As you start to extend the space between your meals it is not uncommon to feel a little uncomfortable. Distract yourself with activity. Go for a walk or call a friend. If the need to munch becomes overwhelming reach for some low carbohydrate vegetables. Avoid potatoes, corn, sweet potatoes, and carrots. We need minerals more than any other nutrient so consider low carbohydrate veggies an unlimited snack food.

One of the reasons you may feel a little uncomfortable is because your stomach is shrinking. While you are losing weight a little light headedness is also normal. Sit down if you feel this way and take it easy. But if this situation becomes a deterrent to your regular activities, you may be hypoglycemic and need to eat more frequently. See your doctor and read Chapter 3.

When considering the size of your portions, know that your stomach *should* be about the size of your fist. When you have eaten enough food to equal the size of your clenched fist, quit.

Note: On the operating room table I have seen average-sized stomachs first-hand. I have also seen stomachs that had been stretched to the size of a watermelon! This is a situation that can become lethal. A larger stomach has a thinner wall and is prone to rupture. Unfortunately, this is also something I have witnessed personally. The patient did not survive.

STEP 4

Increase your Meal Spacing gradually (up to 6 hours maximum) until you reach your goal weight. Ideally, you should increase slowly (no more than 1 hour per week) to give your mind and body time to adjust to this new regimen. After you reach your goal weight, four to five hours between meals is ideal for weight maintenance. Watch for changes in how you feel and function then adjust your diet, activity level, and meal spacing accordingly.

Exercise will alter your metabolism. I have found that vigorous exercise increases my appetite too much, forcing me to have smaller spaces between meals. When we exercise, our bodies need more nutrition to accommodate growing muscles and increased metabolism. This is fine if you are an athlete. But since I am most concerned with health and weight control I try to limit most of my exercise to slow metabolism workouts such as yoga and walking. These activities do not increase my appetite but help to tone, stimulate blood flow, and increase flexibility. With yoga's deep breathing exercises it is also an excellent non-dynamic "aerobic" workout. The body is oxygenated without stress to the ankles, knees, and spine. Remember, slow sustained exercise is not only better for the joints, it is also the best fat-burning exercise.

STEP 5

If you are not exercising at all at this time, begin by walking for a few minutes each day or every other day. Gradually increase the time until you are walking up to one hour per day or try some other low metabolism activity that is within your fitness level, such as swimming, water aerobics, tai chi, or low impact aerobics. If you are intimidated by a classroom situation, try a video or book first. This is an excellent way to start.

Sample Meal Spacing Schedules:

4 HR

7 A.M.	11 A.M.	3 P.M.	7 P.M.	11 P.M.
8 A.M.	12 Noon	4 P.M.	8 P.M.	
9 A.M.	1 P.M.	5 P.M.	9 P.M.	

5 HR

6 A.M.	11 A.M.	4 P.M.	9 P.M.
7 A.M.	12 P.M.	5 P.M.	10 P.M.

Note: Hypoglycemics should eat upon rising and again right at bedtime. This will help prevent the insomnia that is related to a glucose imbalance in the night.

Utilizing this weight loss formula, I no longer have any worries about weight gain. For the first time in my life, I know that weight *control* is within my grasp.

What to Eat:

Whole Grains. Eat 100% whole wheat bread (not enriched), brown rice, and whole grain cereals (limit cereals to those with 7g of sugar or less). White foods deplete energy because the vitamin rich outer husk has been removed. If the nutrients needed for metabolism are not in the food, they will be leached from the body's supply. Eating whole grain foods will increase power, strength, and stamina. Whole grain rice contains antioxidants which have antiaging properties.

Protein. Protein at every meal. Protein builds muscle, relieves aches and pains, and stimulates the release of stored fat. Without enough protein in the diet, production and activity of neurotransmitters and neurohormones will be reduced.

Try to include more white meat (fish and poultry) and soy products than red meat. Also consider dairy for protein and calcium if you are not lactose intolerant. One cup of cottage cheese has twenty-eight grams of protein! An average meal should have approximately fifteen grams of protein to twenty grams of carbohydrate (See Dr. Barry Sears' book *The Zone* to determine your own individual needs. Check the Resources Section of this book for more information).

No carbs eaten without protein at the same time. Prevents blocked fat stores and elevated insulin levels.

Fruit or Vegetable eaten at every meal. Fruit should be limited and eaten preferably first thing in the morning as it digests more quickly than other foods. Hypoglycemics and diabetics may need to eliminate fruit almost entirely because of its high sugar content. I suffer disease symptoms if I eat more than one piece of fruit a day. Fresh vegetables should make up for this deficit, however. Fruits and vegetables add vitamins, antioxidants, and minerals to the diet. Isoflavones, phytochemicals, and amino acids are also essential ingredients for health that can only be found in natural foods. These foods increase clarity, reduce the risk of cancer, and promote longevity.

Limit juice to one glass a day (unsweetened). Vegetable juice, tomato juice, and unsweetened grapefruit juice are acceptable. A glass of juice may contain the sugar and calories of up to eight pieces of fresh fruit!

No Alcohol, Smoking, or Drugs. Adults—moderate alcohol. Preferably dry (rather than sweet) and red wine (rather than white). No more than one glass a day. Hypoglycemics should have no alcohol whatsoever because alcohol lowers blood sugar and may reduce blood glucose to dangerous levels. (See Chapter 16: Alcohol Alternatives, and Chapter 3: How to Quit Smoking.)

No Caffeine. Caffeine is a psychoactive drug (See Chapter 10). It alters the metabolism and, contrary to what you might believe, it depletes energy. It also promotes insomnia, anxiety, and nervous agitation.

Multi-vitamin. Daily. Certain diseases may be prevented with a daily supplement of vitamins and minerals. B-complex vitamins are required to metabolize sugar. If they are not present in your diet they will be depleted from your body's supply. If this happens the brain will have insufficient quantities for normal function resulting in behavioral and cognitive impairment.

Calcium and Iron. Women should take a daily supplement. Calcium affects mood and energy. It also helps prevent osteoporosis. It must be taken with magnesium for proper absorption. So look for a supplement with magnesium also on the label. Recent studies even suggest that a diet rich in calcium may increase fat burning.

Fat. If you are eating a low sugar diet most bad fats will be reduced. But whenever you can, choose broiled or baked over fried. Choose monounsaturated spreads instead of butter. Eat more fish and poultry than red meat and reduce the amount of egg yolks and whole fat dairy products in your diet. Generally, bad fat is solid at room temperature. Don't be afraid of good fats like those found in olive oil, flaxseed, and nuts. Having healthy fat in the diet will reduce your cravings for bad fats.

Did you know that the brain is eighty percent fat—both saturated and unsaturated? Fatty acids are essential for brain function. Thirty percent of your total calories is the recommended daily allowance of fat. To learn more about watching fat in your diet read Susan Powter's *Stop the Insanity.*

Limit Salt. Take nothing in excess. Read your labels. Some items contain more than 1000 mg per serving! In restaurants, ask them to hold the MSG (monosodium glutamate). Salt promotes dehydration, headaches, cramping, and joint pain.

Helpful Hint:
Post **The Wise Diet** someplace where you will be able to read it regularly, such as the bathroom wall. It takes at least six to ten repetitions before information is stored in our long-term memory. A daily reminder will be helpful.

Summary:
As you can see, life can still be rich with flavor and fun. All you have to do is remember the basics:

Whole grain carbohydrates (whenever possible), no refined sugar (to the best of your ability). Look for naturally sweetened or artificially sweetened substitutes. Balance your carbohydrate servings with protein servings. Eat healthy fat substitutes (olive oil, monounsaturated spreads, peanut and almond butter, nuts and seeds). Avoid fatty meat, fried foods, and whole milk products. (A once a month treat is acceptable. I allow myself a cheeseburger, some fried chicken, or a pizza periodically. This once or twice a month indulgence hasn't affected my weight loss one bit!) Limit your egg yolks. Drink a minimum of three 24 oz. bottles of water a day. Avoid caffeine, alcohol, and cigarettes.

Sugar and Tobacco

Your cigarette cravings may also be linked to sugar addiction. I'll bet you didn't know that many tobacco companies use sugar in their manufacturing process. Leaves soaked in a sugar solution are not only considered more flavorful, but they are also more addictive. Ever wonder why you crave sweets when you try to quit smoking?

Just under half a million lives per year are lost to tobacco. That is nearly 1200 deaths per day. Eighty percent of the smoking population say they wish to quit but don't know how. There are several options available. These include nicotine patches, nicotine gum, nicotine inhalers, and sprays. Or you can talk to your doctor about Bupropion Hydrochloride (Zyban), a prescription pill. This option, however, may not work for everyone. Some people should avoid it due to negative side effects.

Here is a *trick* for cutting down without the use of nicotine or drugs. Count the amount of cigarettes that you smoke in a day. Then deplete that number by one per week. In other words, if you smoke a pack a day or twenty cigarettes, the first week cut back to smoking only nineteen cigarettes a day. The second week, eighteen and the third, only seventeen cigarettes a day. It is quite easy to cut back by only one a day per week. By doing this you are gradually decreasing your nicotine addiction.

I was not able to quit smoking "cold turkey" but with this plan I was able to cut down from a pack a day to only five cigarettes a week in a year's time. Then when my husband said, "You're hardly smoking at all. Why don't you just quit?" it was easy to do so.

An occasional "sympathetic smoke" among friends is not healthy but is allowable, as long as you never actually *purchase* another pack. This is your safety catch. Fortunately, these friendly smokes taste nastier each time. Eventually, you'll have the strength to just say no. Remember, it's never too late to quit. The benefits of quitting are enormous. After just one year without cigarettes, your risk of heart disease is reduced by half and after fifteen years your body recovers its health so completely that your risk becomes that of people who have never smoked. It is important to note, however, that secondary smoke is also harmful and should be avoided whenever possible.

Part II

Directory of

Low Sugar Foods

Warning!

Not all diets are suitable for everyone and this or any other diet program may result in variable success. Any user of this program assumes responsibility for the weight loss and health obtained. The author, publisher, and distributors of this book do not specifically endorse any of the products listed, nor do they make any claim that these products or their ingredients are healthful. Not all products listed are safe for diabetics or hypoglycemics. Products may be high in fat or contain ingredients such as aspartame, polyols, or hydrogenated oils that may be hazardous to your health. To reduce risk of health, consult your doctor before beginning this program. This book is not intended to replace medical advice or be a substitute for a physician. If you are taking prescribed medication please consult your physician as any dietary changes will affect the metabolism of that medication. The creators, contributors, and distributors of this program expressly disclaim responsibility for any adverse effects, liabilities, or loss in connection with the advice herein.

Phenylketonurics: many of the products listed contain phenylalanine. People with phenylketonuria (PKU) should not consume phenylalanine. Please read product labels carefully, (See Chapter 1: Aspartame).

Product information is derived from package text. Material in quotations is manufacturer's quote. Author comments are in italics preceding various listings. Not all package information or product ingredients are listed. Accuracy of listings is not guaranteed. Please check each product label carefully, do your own research, and consume products at your own risk. This directory is in no way all inclusive.

Note: A product may contain sweetening agents and fillers that are not required by law to be listed on the package label.

Directory of
Low Sugar Foods

Most of the products listed are readily available at your local grocer, natural foods market, pharmacy or drugstore. If you cannot find a product, check with your store manager. He or she should be able to order the product for you by looking for the company name in the store's distributor catalogue. Prices may vary.

Some of the items listed contain "Sugar Alcohol." This is a term that the FDA requires to be used in the Nutrition Facts panel to list a group of artificial sweeteners that are called "Polyols" (See Chapter 1). These include Maltitol and Isomal, sweeteners that do not contain sugar or alcohol. However, if eaten in excess they may cause a laxative effect due to their slow rate of absorption. Don't let a little abdominal discomfort fool you. These products are still better for your health than their sugary counterparts. In fact, this "problem" is actually a built-in mechanism that helps prevent you from overeating.

Many of the foods listed also contain aspartame, or phenylalanine (See Chapter 1), an ingredient that should be avoided by some persons. People with phenylketonuria (PKU) should not consume phenylalanine. Please read your labels carefully and educate yourself about these ingredients.

Natural foods are almost always a better choice than products with artificial ingredients. However, for some, such as diabetics and hypoglycemics who must limit *all* sugars, artificially sweetened products are the only alternative. I have attempted to include all the foods I have enjoyed: the naturally sweetened lower glycemic options (that do contain some sugar) and the artificially sweetened (safe for diabetics) products that may contain aspartame.

Aspartame is an ingredient that should be avoided by some people. Please read Chapter 1 for more information and do your own research about all the products listed and their ingredients so that you can make informed choices for yourself.

How to Use This Directory

First, read it straight through, scanning each entry. You might be surprised at what you find. Then, go back through and circle those that are of interest to you. You might differentiate by such standards as All-natural, 0 grams of Sugar, Fat Free, or No Aspartame. Then take this list with you to the market. If you have any trouble finding something, ask to have the item ordered for you. Happy Shopping! You are well on your way to a new you.

Percentages are daily values based upon a 2,000-calorie diet.* Your daily values may be higher or lower depending on your calorie needs:

	Calories	2,000	2,500
Total Fat	Less than	65g	80g
Saturated Fat	Less than	20g	25g
Cholesterol	Less than	300mg	300mg
Sodium	Less than	2,400mg	2,400mg
Total Carbohydrates	Less than	300g	375g
Dietary Fiber		25g	30g

*National Food Packaging Standards

Quick Reference List

When You Crave:	Reach for:
Chocolate Brownie	Clif Bar/Chocolate Brownie (Chap. 5)
Chocolate Cake	Sugar-Free Dbl Choc Chip Creme Cake (Chap. 4)
Creme Filled Cakes	Sugar-Free Angel Food Cake (Chap. 20)
Strawberry Shortcake	Sugar-Free Angel Food Cake (Chap. 20)
Carrot Cake	Clif Bar/Carrot Cake (Chap. 5)
Lemon Cake	Lemon Cake (Chap. 4)
Lemon Poppy Seed Muffin	Luna/Lemon Zest (Chap. 5)
Milk Chocolate	Estee, Fifty/50, Tropical Source, Cloud Nine (Chap. 8)
Milk Chocolate with Almonds	Estee, Fifty/50, Tropical Source, Cloud Nine (Chap. 8)
Crisp Rice Chocolate	Estee, Fifty/50, Tropical Source, Cloud Nine (Chap. 8)
Hot Chocolate	Sugar-Free Hot Chocolate (Chap. 10)
Swiss Mocha	General Foods International Coffee (Chap. 10)
French Vanilla Coffee	General Foods International Coffee (Chap. 10)
Ice Cream	Breyers, Edy's, Rice Dream (Chap. 12)
Ice Cream Sandwich	Eskimo Pie, Rice Dream Ice Cream Sandwiches (Chap. 12)
Chocolate Covered Ice Cream	Eskimo Pie, Rice Dream Nut Sundae (Chap. 12)
Tira Misu	Hazelnut Sugar-Free Ice Cream (Chap. 19)
Frozen Fruit Juice Bars	Sugar-Free Fruit Juice Bars (Chap. 12)
Candy Bar (nuts, caramel, choc.)	Epic (Compare to a Snickers® Bar) (Chap.5)
Sandwich Cookies	Frookies (Chap. 4)
Hot fudge Sundae	(See Chapter 19)
Chocolate Chip Cookies	Country Choice, Estee, Fifty/50 (Chap. 4)
Chocolate Almond Fudge	Clif Bar/Chocolate Almond Fudge (Chap. 5)
Chocolate Almond Brownie	Atkins Bar/Chocolate Brownie (Chap. 5)
Ginger Snaps	Clif Bar/Ginger Snaps (Chap. 5)
Chocolate Pecan Pie	Luna Bar/Chocolate Pecan Pie (Chap. 5)
Coconut Pie	Luna Bar/Tropical Twist (Chap. 5)
Black Forest Cake	BioChem/Black Forest Raspberry Swirl (Chap. 5)
Truffles	Russell Stover Truffles (Chap. 6)
Coconut Clusters	Coconut Almondine (Chap. 5, 19)
Fudge	(See Chapter 19)
Caramel Peanut Clusters	Epic Bar, Russell Stover Pecan Delights (Chap. 6)
Peanut Butter Cups	Russell Stover SF Peanut Butter Cups (Chap. 6)
Chocolate Cheesecake	Source/One Choc Cheesecake Bar (Chap. 5)
Gummie Bears	Bear Bites (Chap. 6)
Licorice	All Natural or Sugar-Free Licorice (Chap. 6)

Chapter 4
Bakery Fresh

Breads

FOOD FOR LIFE® EZEKIEL 4:9™ SPROUTED GRAIN BREAD. *Sesame is our favorite.* Other flavors include: Low Sodium, Cinnamon Raisin, and Regular. Organic. 100% Flourless. No preservatives. *Based on the Old Testament scripture . . . "Take also unto thee wheat . . . barley . . . beans . . . lentils . . . millet . . . spelt and put them in one vessel, and make bread of it . . ." EZ 4:9.* Available at health food markets. Net Wt. 24 oz. (1 1/2 lb.) 680g, Serving Size 1 slice (34g), Servings per container 20, Calories 80, Calories from Fat 5, Total Fat 0.5g, Saturated Fat 0g, Cholesterol 0mg, Sodium 75mg, Potassium 80mg, Total Carbohydrate 15g, Dietary Fiber 3g, **Sugars 0g**, Protein 4g, Thiamine 8%, Phosphorus 8%, Riboflavin 2%, Magnesium 6%, Niacin 6%, Zinc 4%, Iron 4%, Vitamin B$_6$ 4%. FOOD FOR LIFE Baking Co., Inc.

FOOD FOR LIFE® EZEKIEL 4:9™ CINNAMON RAISIN SPROUTED GRAIN BREAD. *Organic. 100% Flourless. No preservatives. Organic. Live Grains.* Sweetened with barley malt and raisins. Available at your health food market. Net Wt. 24 oz. (1 1/2 lb.), 680g, Serving Size 1 slice (34g), Servings per container 20, Calories 80, Calories from Fat 5, Total Fat 0.5g, Saturated Fat 0g, Cholesterol 0mg, Sodium 65mg, Potassium 120mg, Total Carbohydrate 18g, Dietary Fiber 2g, **Sugars 5g**, Protein 3g, Thiamine 8%, Phosphorus 6%, Riboflavin 2%, Magnesium 6%, Niacin 6%, Zinc 4%, Iron 4%, Vitamin B$_6$ 4%. FOOD FOR LIFE Baking Co.

The following bread does contain some sugar but is often the best choice available as it is 100% Stone Ground Whole Wheat:

PEPPERIDGE FARM® NATURAL WHOLE GRAIN BREAD, 9 GRAIN. *"Delicious Taste & Texture from 9 Grains", Double Wrapped. Low Fat. No artificial ingredients or preservatives. No Cholesterol.* Sweetened with raisin juice concentrate, high fructose corn syrup, unsulphured molasses, and honey. Available at most grocery stores. Net Wt. 24 oz. (1.5 Lbs.) (680g), Serving Size 1 Slice (34g/ 1.2 oz.), Servings 20, Calories 90, Calories from Fat 10, Total

Fat 1g, Saturated Fat 0g, Cholesterol 0mg, Sodium 140mg, Total Carbohydrate 15g, Dietary Fiber 3g, **Sugars 2g**, Protein 4g, Calcium 4%, Thiamin 4%, Niacin 4%, Iron 4%, Folate 2%. PEPPERIDGE FARM, INC.

At the regular market I often choose this brand. Although it contains some sugar and "enriched wheat flour" it is still full of crunchy good things . . . walnuts, wheat germ, sunflower seeds, oatmeal, rye barley, and corn meal. I love it!:

BROWNBERRY® HEALTH NUT BREAD.
"Eat right–Feel Good" Natural. Catherine Clark's original recipe. Sweetened with brown sugar and honey. Net Wt. 1 lb. (453g), Serving Size 1 Slice (25g), Servings 18, Calories 70, Calories from Fat 15, Total Fat 1.5g, Saturated Fat 0g, Cholesterol 0mg, Sodium 150mg, Total Carbohydrate 12g, Dietary Fiber 1g, **Sugars 2g**, Protein 2g, Iron 2%. BROWNBERRY, a division of ARNOLD FOODS CO. INC.

Cakes

Most grocery stores will have sugar-free cakes and pies in their bakery department. During the holidays our favorite is sugar-free pumpkin pie. Some stores even have specialty cakes such as cheesecake or ice cream cakes available in low-sugar versions. Many will make sugar-free cakes to order including chocolate layer cakes or frosted and decorated cakes for birthdays and other special occasions. Don't be afraid to ask and order.

FEARN® SPICE CAKE MIX.
Made with Organically Grown Stoneground Whole Wheat. Also available: Carrot Cake, Banana Cake, and Carob Cake. Available at your health foods market. Net Wt. 8.6 oz. (244g). Add honey or barley malt syrup for sweetening. FEARN NATURAL FOODS, A Division of Modern Products, Inc.

ANGEL FOOD CAKE.
Sweetened with Maltitol. Available in the bakery department of most grocery stores. Net Wt. 9 oz. (255g), Serving size 1/5 of cake (51g), Servings per container 5, Calories 90, Calories from Fat 0, Total Fat 0g, Saturated Fat 0g, Polyunsaturated Fat 0g, Cholesterol 0mg, Sodium 370mg, Total Carbohydrate 29g, Dietary Fiber 3g, **Sugars 0g**, Sugar Alcohols 14g, Protein 3g, Calcium 6%. SPECIAL TOUCH BAKERIES, Inc.

APPLE COFFEE CRUMB CAKE – NO SUGAR ADDED
"A moist coffee cake made with real apple juice." Sweetened with Lactitol, apples, and apple juice. Check the bakery department of your local grocer. Net Wt. 13 oz. (369g), Serving Size 1 piece, Servings per container 5, Calories 120, Calories from Fat 60, Total Fat 5g, Saturated Fat 1g, Cholesterol 30mg, Sodium

180mg, Total Carbohydrate 21g, **Sugar 0.5g,** Protein 2g, Iron 2%. BUTTERFLY BAKERY.

SUGAR FREE DOUBLE CHOCOLATE CHIP CREME CAKE.
"A moist creme cake with sugar-free chocolate chips" Sweetened with Lactitol and Maltitol. Available in the bakery department of most grocery stores. Net Wt. 12 oz. (340g), Serving Size 1 Pc (68g), Servings Per Container 5, Amount Per Serving: Calories 120, Calories From Fat 60, Total Fat 5g, Saturated Fat 1g, Cholesterol 30mg, Sodium 180mg, Total Carbohydrate 21g, **Sugars 0g,** Protein 2g, Iron 2%. BUTTERFLY BAKERY.

Cookies
HAIN PURE FOODS KIDZ™ All Natural ANIMAL COOKIES.
No artificial flavors, colors or preservatives. Reduced Fat – 50% Less Fat than the leading brand. No hydrogenated oils. Naturally sweetened with dehydrated cane juice and cane juice syrup. Net Wt. 17 oz. (482g), Serving size 9 cookies (28g), Servings per container about 17, Calories 120, Calories from Fat 20, Total Fat 2g, Saturated Fat 0.5g, Cholesterol 0mg, Sodium 80mg, Total Carbohydrate 23g, **Sugars 6g,** Protein 2g, Iron 4%. Manufactured for distribution by: THE HAIN FOOD GROUP, Inc.

ESTEE® Fructose Sweetened CHOCOLATE CHIP COOKIES.
Low Sodium. Sweetened with fructose. Net Wt. 7oz. (198g), Serving size 4 cookies, Servings per box 6, Calories 160, Calories from Fat 70, Total Fat 8g, Saturated Fat 2g, Cholesterol 0mg, Sodium 40mg, Total Carbohydrate 21g, Dietary Fiber 1g, **Sugars 6g,** Protein 2g, Iron 4%. THE HAIN FOOD GROUP, Inc. *Sponsor of the American Diabetes Association®.*

A single wrapped cookie. Delicious and nutritious:

BIOCHEM® Sports & Fitness Systems ULTIMATE PROTEIN COOKIE – CHOCOLATE COFFEE CRUNCH. Other flavors include: Chocolate Chip and Chocolate Peanut Butter. Sweetened with Maltitol, fructose, Maltodextrin. Net Wt. 1.9 oz. (56g), Serving Size 1 Cookie, Calories 180, Calories from Fat 30, Total Fat 3g, Saturated Fat 3g, Cholesterol 5mg, Sodium 25mg, Potassium 105mg, Total Carbohydrate 10g, **Sugars 2g,** Protein 21g, and 60% of 19 Vitamins and Minerals. BIOCHEM.

ESTEE® Fructose Sweetened LEMON COOKIES.
Natural & Artificially Flavored. Low Sodium. Sweetened with fructose. Net Wt. 7oz. (198g), Serving size 4 cookies, Servings per box 6, Calories 160, Calories from Fat 70, Total Fat 8g, Saturated Fat 2g, Cholesterol 0mg, Sodium 40mg, Total Carbohydrate 20g, Dietary Fiber 2g, **Sugars 6g,** Protein 2g, Iron 4%. THE HAIN FOOD GROUP, Inc., *A proud sponsor of the American Diabetes Association.*®

Simply the best chocolate chip cookies I've found:

COUNTRY CHOICE® Certified Organic Soft Baked CHOCOLATE CHIP WALNUT COOKIES. *Wheat Free. Milk Free. No Hydrogenated Oils. No Refined Sweeteners. No Artificial Flavors, Colors, or Preservatives.* Other flavors include: Double Fudge Brownie, Oatmeal Chocolate Chip, Oatmeal Raisin, Peanut Butter, Rocky Road, Ginger, Southern Pecan Shortbread. Sweetened with evaporated cane juice, cane syrup, and honey. Net Wt. 7.25 oz. (206g), Serving Size 1 cookie (23g), Servings 9, Calories 100, Fat Calories 35, Total Fat 3.5g, Saturated Fat 1.5g, Cholesterol 5mg, Sodium 65mg, Total Carbohydrate 15g, Dietary Fiber 1g, **Sugars 10g**, Protein 1g, Iron 2%. COUNTRY CHOICE NATURALS.

FIFTY 50® Fructose Sweetened CHOCOLATE CHIP COOKIES. Other flavors: Coconut, Oatmeal, Butter, Fudge. A low glycemic food. Sweetened with crystalline fructose. The chocolate chips are sweetened with Maltitol. Net Wt. 7 oz. (198g), Serving size 4 cookies (32g), Servings per container 6, Calories 170, Calories from Fat 80, Total Fat 9g, Saturated Fat 2.5g, Cholesterol 0mg, Sodium 35mg, Total Carbohydrate 20g, **Sugars 6g**, Maltitol 2g, Protein 2, Vitamin A 2%, Calcium 6%, Iron 4%. FIFTY 50 FOODS, *One-half of all profits fund Diabetes research. To date, contributions have totaled over $5 million.*

FIFTY 50® CHOCOLATE CREME FILLED WAFERS. A low-glycemic food. Sweetened with Sorbitol, Maltodextrin, and aspartame. Net Wt. 3.5 oz. (99g), Serving size 6 Wafers (31g), Servings 3, Calories 160, Calories from Fat 80, Total Fat 9g, Saturated Fat 2g, Cholesterol 0mg, Sodium 45mg, Total Carbohydrate 20g, **Sugars 0g**, Sorbitol 7g, Protein 2g, Calcium 2%, Iron 4%. FIFTY 50 FOODS. *One-half of all profits fund Diabetes research. To date, contributions have totaled over five million dollars.*

SWEET'N LOW® Sugar-Free Brand CHOCOLATEY WAFER BARS. *Individually wrapped. 40% Fewer Calories. "45% Less Fat than the average of the leading chocolate candy brands."* Sweetened with Lactitol, Isomalt, Polydextrose. Net Wt. 2.75 oz. (78g), Serving Size 3 Bars (47g), Servings 2, Calories 140, Calories from Fat 60, Total Fat 7g, Saturated Fat 6g, Cholesterol 0mg, Sodium 100mg, Total Carbohydrate 23g, Dietary Fiber 1g, **Sugars 0g**, Sugar Alcohol 11g, Protein 4g, Calcium 2%, Iron 2%. *"Benefat,™ also known as 'salatrim,' is a real fat made from vegetable oil and other components normally found in the diet. It has all the taste, texture and mouthfeel of traditional fats, but with 45% fewer calories. Only 55% of Benefat™ is absorbed by the body as fat."* SIMPLY LITE® FOODS CORP.

Compare to Oreo® Brand Sandwich Cookies:

ALL NATURAL FROOKIE® FROOKWICH® SANDWICH COOKIES.
The Good For You Cookie® All natural. No cholesterol. Low Fat–2g Fat per cookie. Sweetened with naturally milled sugar and molasses. DUPLEX Chocolate & Vanilla Sandwich Cookies: Net Wt. 11 oz. (311g), Serving Size 3 cookies (33g), Servings 9, Calories 150, Fat Calories 50, Total Fat 6g, Saturated Fat 0.5g, Polyunsaturated Fat 2g, Monounsaturated Fat 3.5g, Cholesterol 0mg, Sodium 95mg, Total Carbohydrate 23g, Dietary Fiber 2g, **Sugars 10g**, Protein 2g, Calcium 4%, Iron 6%. DELICIOUS BRAND, INC.

There's only one problem with these cookies . . . who can eat only two? They are amazing:

JENNIES® COCONUT MACAROONS.
100% Natural. No Synthetic Color, No Artificial Flavor, and No Chemical Preservatives. Gluten Free, Lactose Free, Wheat Free, Sulfite Free. Source of MCT's for energy. Best Source of: Lauric and Capric Acid. Ingredients: Unsweetened coconut, honey, & egg whites. Net Wt. 8 oz. (226g), Serving Size 2 Cookies (30g), Servings 9, Calories 130, Fat Calories 60, Total Fat 7g, Saturated Fat 6g, Cholesterol 0mg, Sodium 10mg, Total Carbohydrate 17g, Dietary Fiber 3g, **Sugars 15g,** Protein 1g, Iron 2%. RED MILL FARMS® INC. *Established 1919.*

PAMELA'S® CHOCOLATE CHIP SHORTBREAD WITH PECANS.
Gourmet All Natural Cookies. Wheat and Egg Free & Gluten Free. "delicate buttery cookie made with rice flour . . . rich, dark semi sweet chunks... pecan pieces... create an incredibly decadent cookie . . . because no one should be denied the pleasure of eating cookies!" Also available are biscotti and baking mixes. Other cookie flavors include: Shortbread Swirl, Peanut Butter, Carob Hazelnut, Chocolate Double Chip, Chunky Chocolate Chip, Butter Shortbread, Ginger, Oatmeal Date Coconut, Pecan Shortbread, and Lemon Shortbread. Sweetened with molasses, honey, rice syrup, and grape juice concentrate.Net Wt. 7.25 oz. (206g), Serving Size 1 Cookie (23g), Servings 9, Calories 130, Calories from Fat 65, Total Fat 7g, Saturated Fat 4g, Cholesterol 15mg, Sodium 60mg, Total Carbohydrate 15g, Dietary Fiber 2%, **Sugars 5g,** Protein 1g, Vitamin A 6%. PAMELA'S PRODUCTS, INC.

ARCHWAY® HOME STYLE COOKIES.
Soft Cookies. Many Flavors. No Sugar. No Cholesterol. Sweetened with Sorbitol and Maltitol. LEMON: Net Wt. 6.75 oz. (191g), Serving Size 1 cookie (24g), Servings 8, Calories 110, Fat Calories 45, Total Fat 5g, Saturated Fat 1g, Monounsaturated Fat 2g, Cholesterol 0mg, Sodium 45mg, Total Carbohydrate 16g, Dietary

Fiber 0g, **Sugars 0g,** Sugar Alcohols 7g, Protein 1g, Iron 2%. ARCHWAY COOKIES, INC. *A Proud Sponsor of the American Diabetes Association®.*

MURRAY® Sugar-Free CHOCOLATE SANDWICH COOKIES.
Sweetened with Sorbitol, Lactitol, Polydextrose, Maltodextrin, aspartame. Net Wt. 6.5 oz. (184g), Serving Size 3 cookies (28g), Servings per container 7, Calories 120, Calories from Fat 50, Total Fat 6g, Saturated Fat 1.5g, Cholesterol 0mg, Sodium 90mg, Total Carbohydrate 19g, **Sugars 0g**, Sugar Alcohol 5g, Protein 2g, Iron 2%. MURRAY BISCUIT COMPANY, LLC.

MURRAY® Sugar-Free VANILLA WAFERS.
Sweetened with Sorbitol, Lactitol, polydextrose, Maltodextrin, aspartame. Net Wt. 5.5 oz. (156g), Serving Size 9 cookies (31g), Servings per container 5, Calories 120, Calories from Fat 35, Total Fat 4g, Saturated Fat 1g, Cholesterol 0mg, Sodium 85mg, Total Carbohydrate 23g, **Sugars 0g**, Sugar Alcohol 8g, Protein 2g, Iron 2%. MURRAY BISCUIT COMPANY, LLC.

VOORTMAN® Sugar-Free VANILLA WAFERS.
Sweetened with Sorbitol and aspartame. Net Wt. 9 oz. (255g), Serving Size 3 cookies (30g), Servings 10, Calories 160, Fat Calories 100, Total Fat 11g, Saturated Fat 2.5g, Cholesterol 0mg, Sodium 30mg, Total Carbohydrate 18g, **Sugars 0g,** Protein <1g, Iron 2%. VOORTMAN COOKIES LTD.

Crackers

AK-MAK® 100% Whole Wheat Stone Ground SESAME CRACKERS.
Low Fat. No Cholesterol. California State Fair Blue Ribbon . . .Gold Medallion Winner. No Preservatives, Bleaches, or Bromates. Includes Bran, Germ, and Endosperm. Sweetened with clover honey. Net Wt. 4.15 oz. (118g), Serving size 5 crackers, Servings per container 4, Calories 116, Calories from Fat 20, Total Fat 2.27g, Saturated Fat 0.48g, Cholesterol 0mg, Sodium 213mg, Total Carbohydrate 19g, Dietary Fiber 3.5g, **Sugars 2.28g,** Protein 4.61g, Iron 6%. AK-MAK BAKERIES.

Chapter 5
Bars

For a long time I thought that if it was labeled "energy" "power," or "diet," it was good for me. It wasn't until I began to investigate hypoglycemia and the refined sugar connection that I began to notice the high amounts of added sugar in these products. Many of these products are now "off limits." But a few good options remain. Remember, the first rule is always to check the label for added sugar. Check the grams if you are unsure and be aware that naturally sweetened products usually do metabolize more slowly than products sweetened with refined sugar. However, just because a product is sweetened naturally does not mean you can have all you want. Tolerances will vary but be sure to count sugar grams both natural and refined.

Consider this scale:

Three to seven grams per serving is the maximun level desired for refined sugar sweetened products. (The Sugar Busters! gang suggests only one to three grams) If you are having symptoms of any kind, limit products with refined sugars to three grams of sugar per serving or less.

Note: A product does not have to taste sweet to have this much added sugar and even small amounts of real sugar may cause symptoms and/or addiction. Check the label for added sugar. (See How to Find Sugar on the Label, Chapter 1).

Zero to twelve grams of natural sugar are great but, hypoglycemics should be wary of using low carbohydrate bars as meal replacements as they may not deliver enough carbohydrates to maintain glucose balance between meals.

Thirteen to twenty grams of sugar per serving is okay for naturally sweetened products but not for refined sugar sweetened products. Twelve grams or above per serving of any sugar, however, may cause symptoms in hypoglycemics. If you are having any symptoms at all, limit naturally sweetened products to no more than twelve grams of sugar per serving. Natural sugars are better tolerated than refined sugars because of the slower rate of absorption into the blood stream but must still be limited.

Over twenty grams of sugar in a product usually means that it has refined sugar and should be avoided. Even natural food products, however, can be a problem. Consider fruit juice, which may have the sugar content of up to eight pieces of fruit in a single glass. Juice is highly condensed and should be avoided by hypoglycemics.

Maximum sugar intake:
Naturally sweetened – 12 grams of sugar per serving
Refined sugars – 3 grams of sugar per serving

Note: Your results may vary. Every individual's specific response to food and nutritional requirements are unique. Age, health, genetic predisposition, emotional wellbeing, and environmental factors must all be considered. These numbers, which are based on the author's personal medical history, are to be used as a guideline only. See your physician to determine your own individual tolerances.

Diet & Energy

Honestly, I haven't yet found a "diet" bar that is low in sugar, although naturally sweetened energy bars abound. When selecting a bar, be sure to check the label for sugar grams. Since I am hypoglycemic, I divide bars that have more than twelve grams of sugar in half, unless I am actively involved in a vigorous activity such as biking or hiking.

I love this one. Doesn't melt. Great for hiking. You can order it in bulk off their web-site:

BALANCE OUTDOOR™ CHOCOLATE CRISP.
The All Natural Energy Bar for Sustained Energy. The low sugar version of the Jenny Craig and Balance Bars. Great for outdoor use—no chocolate coating to melt. Does not contain soy protein from genetically modified soy. Balanced 40-30-30. Protein 15g. Sweetened with Mixed Fruit

Juice Concentrates, Natural Grain Dextrins, Honey, Organic Agave Nectar, and Organic Brown Rice Syrup. Other flavors include: Crunchy Peanut, Honey Almond, and Nut berry. Net Wt. 1.76 oz., 1 Bar (50g), Total Fat 6g, Saturated Fat 1.5g, Cholesterol 5mg, Sodium 140mg, Potassium 260mg, Total Carbohydrate 21g, Dietary Fiber 3g, **Sugar 12g**, Protein 15g, Calcium 8% D.V., Iron 15% D.V. BALANCE BAR COMPANY. *Your purchase helps plant American Forests Global Releaf* trees to restore forest habitat.* May be purchased individually per bar at retailer locations or in quantity from the website www.balance.com (15 bars per box).

Just look at all the healthy ingredients in this bar . . . it truly is like taking a multi-vitamin:

CLIF BAR® COOKIES 'N CREAM.
Many other flavors are available including Cranberry apple cherry, Apricot, Chocolate chip, Chocolate brownie, Chocolate chip peanut crunch, Chocolate almond fudge, Ginger snap, Crunchy peanut butter, and Carrot cake. *Nutrition for sustained energy. Non-GMO soy protein. 23 Vitamins & Minerals. "Here's the energy you need for the long haul . . . has been shown to help sustain energy levels without a sugar crash." Whole grains and fruit. Wheat and Dairy free. 100% Natural.* Sweetened with Brown Rice Syrup, Evaporated Cane Juice, Malt Extract, Apple Net Wt. 2.4 oz. (68g), Serving size 1 bar, Calories 230, Calories from Fat 30, Total Fat 3.5g, Saturated Fat 1.5g, Cholesterol 0mg, Sodium 180mg, Potassium 210mg, Total Carbohydrate 39g, Dietary Fiber 5g, **Sugars 21g**, Other Carbohydrate 11g, Protein 10g, Vitamin A 30%, Vitamin C 100%, Calcium 30%, Iron 30%, Vitamin E 100%, Vitamin K 20%, Thiamin (B_1) 25%, Riboflavin (B_2) 15%, Niacin (B_3) 15%, Vitamin B_6 20%, Folate 20%, Vitamin B_{12} 15%, Biotin 15%, Pantothenic Acid 20%, Phosphorus 25%, Iodine 15%, Magnesium 25%, Zinc 20%, Selenium 20%, Copper 25%, Manganese 30%, Chromium 20%, Molybdemum 15%. Fiber, Fig Paste. CLIF BAR, INC.

A nutritional snack bar made just for women . . . can you believe it? They taste great too:

LUNA™ CHOCOLATE PECAN PIE.
Available in eight other flavors including S'mores, Nuts over chocolate, Lemon zest, Tropical crisp, Chai tea, Toasted nuts 'n cranberry, and Sesame raisin crunch. *A whole nutrition bar created especially for women. Voted Best New Product of 1999 by the food industry. ". . . cross between a Rice Crispies Treat and a chewy granola bar," Cooking Light Magazine Jan/Feb 2000. "the Luna can also double as a multivitamin," Good Housekeeping December 1999. Contains calcium, protein, antioxidants, folic acid, minerals, and soy. Wheat and Dairy Free. Made with non-GMO soy.* Sweetened with brown rice syrup and evaporated cane juice. Net Wt.

1 Bar (48g), Calories 180, Calories from Fat 40, Total Fat 4.5g, Saturated Fat 3g, Polyunsaturated Fat 0.5g, Monounsaturated Fat 1g, Cholesterol 0mg, Sodium 125mg, Potassium 105mg, Total Carbohydrates 24g, Dietary Fiber 2g, **Sugars 12g**, Other Carbohydrates 10g, Protein 10g, Vitamin A 25%, Vitamin C 100%, Calcium 35%, Iron 35%, Vitamin E 100%, Vitamin K 100%, Thiamin (B_1) 100%, Riboflavin (B_2) 100%, Niacin (B_3) 100%, Vitamin B_6 100%, Vitamin B_{12} 100%, Biotin 100%, Pantothenic Acid 100%, Phosphorus 35%, Iodine 35%, Zinc 35%, Selenium 35%, Magnesium 35%, Copper 35%, Manganese 35%, Chromium 35%, Molybdenum 35%. CLIF BAR, INC. *A portion of the proceeds generated by sales of this bar are donated to The Breast Cancer Fund.*™

NATURE'S PLUS® THE ENERGY SUPPLEMENTS®
CHINESE HERBAL BAR–100% NATURAL
Supercharged with Whole Foods, Vitamins, & Minerals. Rich Date-Nut Blend. No Cholesterol. High Fiber. Sweetened with fruit. Net Wt. 1.5 oz. (42g), Calories 149, Fat Calories 36, Total Fat 4g, Saturated Fat 0g, Cholesterol 0mg, Sodium 57mg, Potassium 20mg, Total Carbohydrate 20g, Dietary Fiber 5g, **Sugars 7g,** Protein 6g, and up to 200% of 20 vitamins and minerals. NATURE'S PLUS.

High Protein

These bars are great if you have to skip a meal. They contain a good ratio of carbs to protein:

BIO-CHEM® SPORTS & FITNESS SYSTEMS ULTIMATE PROTEIN BAR.™ Available at health food markets. Sweetened with rice syrup, fructose, Polydextrose, turbinado sugar. CHOCOLATE PEANUT BUTTER SUPREME: Net Wt. 40g (1.4 oz.), Serving Size 1 bar, Calories 150, Calories from Fat 30, Total Fat 3.5g, Saturated Fat 2g, Cholesterol 0mg, Sodium 25mg, Potassium 55mg, Total Carbohydrate 10g, Dietary Fiber 0g, **Sugars 6g,** Protein 16g, and 10–50% DV of 19 Vitamins and minerals. BIO-CHEM.

BIO-CHEM® ULTIMATE PROTEIN BAR.™ High Protein, Low Fat Supplement Bar. Available at health food markets. Sweetened with rice syrup, fructose, Polydextrose, turbinado sugar. CHOCOLATE, CHOCOLATE DREAM: Net Wt. 40g (1.4 oz.), Serving Size 1 bar, Calories 140, Calories from Fat 25, Total Fat 2.5g, Saturated Fat 1.5g, Cholesterol 0mg, Sodium 30mg, Potassium 95mg, Total Carbohydrate 10g, Dietary Fiber 0g, **Sugars 6g,** Protein 15g, and 10 – 50% DV of 19 vitamins and minerals. COUNTRY LIFE.

BIO-CHEM® ULTIMATE PROTEIN BAR.™ High Protein, Low Fat Supplement Bar. Sweetened with turbinado sugar, fructose, and sugar. Available at health foods markets. CHEWY CHOCOLATE CHIP: Net Wt. 40g (1.4 oz.), Serving Size 1 bar, Calories 150, Calories from Fat 30, Total Fat 3g, Saturated Fat 2g,

Cholesterol 0mg, Sodium 20mg, Potassium 35mg, Total Carbohydrate 10g, Dietary Fiber 0g, **Sugars 8g**, Protein 15g, and 2–50% of 19 vitamins and minerals. BIOCHEM.

MET-RX® SOURCE/ONE™ NUTRITIONAL FOOD BAR.

"Engineered Nutrition," High Protein. High Calcium – 50% Recommended Daily Allowance. High in Antioxidants. Low Fat. Low Fructose/Sucrose. Sweetened with brown rice syrup, rice syrup, Maltitol, and Polydextrose. CHOCOLATE CHEESECAKE BAR. Net Wt. 2.2 oz. (62.5g), Serving Size 1 Bar, Calories 190, Calories from Fat 25, Total Fat 3g, Saturated Fat 2.5g, Cholesterol 0mg, Sodium 40mg, Potassium 400mg, Total Carbohydrate 30g, Dietary Fiber 1g, **Sugars 4g,** Sugar Alcohols 12g, Protein 15g, and 20%–340% of 12 vitamins and minerals. MET-RX USA, INC.

MET-RX® PROTEIN PLUS™ HIGH PROTEIN FOOD BAR.

32 Grams of Protein. Only 15 Grams of Carbohydrates. Sweetened with malt barley syrup, Maltitol, Sucralose, and Polydextrose CHOCOLATE ROASTED PEANUT: Net Wt. 3 oz. (85g), Serving Size 1 Bar, Calories 260, Calories from Fat 80, Total Fat 8g, Saturated Fat 6g, Cholesterol 5mg, Sodium 85mg, Potassium 120mg, Total Carbohydrate 15g, Dietary Fiber 1g, **Sugars 4g,** Protein 32g, and 25%–100% of 19 vitamins and minerals. MET-RX USA, INC.

MET-RX® PROTEIN PLUS™ HIGH PROTEIN FOOD BAR.

32 Grams of Protein. Only 15 Grams of Carbohydrates. Sweetened with malt barley syrup, Maltitol, Sucralose, and Polydextrose. CHOCOLATE FUDGE: Net Wt. 3 oz. (85g), Serving Size 1 Bar, Calories 260, Calories from Fat 70, Total Fat 8g, Saturated Fat 8g, Cholesterol 5mg, Sodium 85mg, Potassium 120mg, Total Carbohydrate 15g, Dietary Fiber 1g, **Sugars 2g,** Protein 32g, and 25%–100% of 19 vitamins and minerals. MET-RX USA, INC.

PREMIER NUTRITION® ELITE.™

2 Grams of Carbs High Protein Bar. Sweetened with Maltitol Syrup, High Fructose Corn Syrup, and Dextrose. CHOCOLATE PEANUT: Net Wt. 1.4 oz. (41g), Serving Size 1 Bar, Calories 160, Fat Calories 40, Total Fat 4.5g, Saturated Fat 2.5g, Cholesterol 0mg, Sodium 120mg, Total Carbohydrate 2g, Dietary Fiber 1g, **Sugars 2g,** Protein 18g, Calcium 10%, Phosphorus 10%, Iron 4%, Vitamin B_{12} 6%. PREMIER NUTRITION.

This bar contains some sugar but I have included it because of its rich supply of nutrients and high protein content. It is a better choice than a candy bar but, be cautious:

TWIN LAB® SOY SENSATIONS™ CHOCOLATE FONDUE.

Crispy Soy Treat. Wholesome Heart Food. With Folic Acid and 60mg Soy Isoflavones. No Cholesterol. High in Fiber. Sweetened with honey, sugar,

Maltitol Syrup, malt syrup, Dextrose. Net Wt. 1.76 oz. (50g), Serving Size 1 Bar, Calories 180, Fat Calories 50, Total Fat 6g, Saturated Fat 2.5g, Cholesterol 0mg, Sodium 200mg, Potassium 180mg, Total Carbohydrate 22g, Dietary Fiber 5g, **Sugars 11g**, Protein 15g, Calcium 6%, Phosphorus 15%, Iron 10%, Zinc 4%, Vitamin E 150%, Copper 10%, Folic Acid 100%, Manganese 10%. Distributed by: TWIN LABORATORIES, INC.

Low Carbohydrate

ATKINS DIET ADVANTAGE BAR™ ALMOND BROWNIE.
Low Carb Food Bar. Other flavors include: Chunky peanut butter, Chocolate peanut butter, Chocolate coconut, Chocolate raspberry, Praline crunch. Sweetened with Sucralose. Available at natural foods markets. Net Wt. 60g, Serving Size 1 Bar, Calories 230, Fat Calories 90, Total Fat 10g, Saturated Fat 3.3g, Cholesterol 3.1mg, Sodium 223mg, Potassium 600mg, Total Carbohydrate 2.6g, Fiber 2g, **Sugars 0g**, Protein 20g, and 37% to 72% of 19 Vitamins and Minerals. ATKINS NUTRITIONALS, INC.

BIO CHEM® SPORTS & FITNESS SYSTEMS ULTIMATE LO CARB 2 BAR. Other flavors include: Chocolate peanut butter & jam and Coconut almond delight. *High Protein 20g. Chocolate Covered. Soy Protein.* Sweetened with Polydextrose, Maltitol, Xylitol, and Sucralose. BLACK FOREST-RASPBERRY SWIRL Net Wt. 60g (2.1 oz.), Serving size 1 bar, Calories 230, Calories from Fat 60, Total Fat 7g, Saturated Fat 3g, Cholesterol 5mg, Sodium 180mg, Potassium 70mg, Total Carbohydrate 3g, **Sugars 1g**, Protein 20g, Copper 80%, Zinc 70%, Vitamin A 70%, Calcium 10%, Vitamin C 70%, Iron 10%, Vitamin E 70%, Riboflavin 70%, Vitamin B_6 70%, Thiamin 70%, Niacin 70%, Folic Acid 70%, Vitamin B_{12} 80%, Vitamin D 70%, Pantothenic Acid 70%, Iodine 70%, Biotin 70%, Phosphorus 20%, Magnesium 2%.BIO CHEM.

BIO CHEM® SPORTS & FITNESS SYSTEMS ULTIMATE LO CARB BAR.™ Other flavors include: Creamy peanut butter, Chocolate brownie nut, Cool cappucino, Honey almond. *High Protein 20g. Chocolate Covered. Soy Protein. ALL NATURAL.* Sweetened with Stevia. Purchase at the natural foods market. AMARETTO IRISH CREAM: Net Wt 60g (2.1 oz), Serving size 1 bar, Calories 240, Calories from Fat 60, Total Fat 6g, Saturated Fat 1g, Cholesterol 20mg, Sodium 360mg, Potassium 90mg, Total Carbohydrate 2g, **Sugars 1g**, Protein 21g, Copper 8%, Vitamin A 90%, Calcium 15%, Vitamin C 90%, Vitamin D 90%, Iron 10%, Vitamin E 90%, Riboflavin 90%, Vitamin B6 90%, Thiamin 90%, Niacin 90%, Folate 90%, Vitamin B_{12} 100%, Vitamin D 90%, Pantothenic Acid 90%, Iodine 90%, Biotin 100%, Phosphorus 30%, Zinc 90%. BIO CHEM.

WORLDWIDE SPORT NUTRITION® PURE PROTEIN™ SPORTS BAR. *High Protein/Low Carb Meal Replacement Bar! Fortified with vitamins and minerals! 20,000mg Amino Acids! Rated Low Glycemic by the Glycemic Research Institute, Washington, D.C. As seen on TV—America's*

Personal Trainer™, *Tony Little*™ Sweetened with Maltitol and Sucralose. PEANUT BUTTER: Net Wt. 50g, Serving Size 1 Bar, Calories 180, Fat Calories 35, Total Fat 4g, Saturated Fat 2g, Cholesterol 3mg, Sodium 60mg, Potassium 80mg, Total Carbohydrate 6g, Dietary Fiber 0g, **Sugars 1.5g**, Protein 21g, and 10–50% of 19 vitamins and minerals. WORLDWIDE SPORT NUTRITIONAL SUPPLEMENTS.

PREMIER NUTRITION® ELITE™ HIGH PROTEIN BAR. 2 Grams of Carbs, Sweetened with Maltitol Syrup, High Fructose Corn Syrup, and Dextrose. CHOCOLATE PEANUT: Net Wt 1.4 oz (41g), Serving Size 1 Bar, Calories 160, Fat Calories 40, Total Fat 4.5g, Saturated Fat 2.5g, Cholesterol 0mg, Sodium 120mg, Total Carbohydrate 2g, Dietary Fiber 1g, **Sugars 2g**, Protein 18g, Calcium 10%, Phosphorus 10%, Iron 4%, Vitamin B12 6%. PREMIER NUTRITION.

WORLDWIDE SPORT NUTRITION® PURE PROTEIN™ SPORTS BAR. *High Protein/Low Carb Meal Replacement Bar! Fortified with vitamins and minerals! 20,000mg Amino Acids! Rated Low Glycemic by the Glycemic Research Institute, Washington, D .C. As seen on TV—America's Personal Trainer,*™ *Tony Little.*™ Sweetened with Maltitol and Sucralose. CHOCOLATE DELUXE: Net Wt. 50g, Serving Size 1 Bar, Calories 180, Fat Calories 30, Total Fat 3.5g, Saturated Fat 2g, Cholesterol 3mg, Sodium 60mg, Potassium 160mg, Total Carbohydrate 9g, Dietary Fiber 1g, **Sugars 1.5g**, Protein 21g, and 10 to 50% of 19 vitamins and minerals. WORLDWIDE SPORT NUTRITIONAL SUPPLEMENTS.

WORLDWIDE SPORT NUTRITION® PURE PROTEIN™ SPORTS BAR. *High Protein/Low Carb Meal Replacement Bar! Fortified with vitamins and minerals! 20,000mg Amino Acids! Rated Low Glycemic by the Glycemic Research Institute, Washington, D. C. As seen on TV—America's Personal Trainer,*™ *Tony Little.*™ Sweetened with Maltitol and Sucralose. WHITE CHOCOLATE MOUSSE: Net Wt. 50g, Serving Size 1 Bar, Calories 190, Fat Calories 35, Total Fat 4g, Saturated Fat 2g, Cholesterol 3mg, Sodium 25mg, Potassium 80mg, Total Carbohydrate 10g, Dietary Fiber 0g, **Sugars 3g**, Protein 22g, and 10–50% of 19 vitamins and minerals. WORLDWIDE SPORT NUTRITIONAL SUPPLEMENTS.

Snack & Granola

Any of the bars listed may be eaten as snacks. But these bars are especially worthy of being listed as treats. (See also Chapter 8: Chocolate.)

BARBARA'S NATURE'S CHOICE® 100% NATURAL LEMON YOGURT DIPPED DESSERTS. Other Barbara's flavors include: Roasted Peanut and Coconut Almond. Sweetened with agave nectar, barley malt extract, evaporated cane juice, Brown Rice Syrup, dehydrated cane juice.

Available at natural foods markets. Net Wt. 6.35 oz. (180g), Serving Size 1 bar (30g), Servings 6, Calories 120, Calories from Fat 30, Total Fat 3.5g, Saturated Fat 2.5g, Cholesterol 0mg, Sodium 10mg, Total Carbohydrate 22g, Dietary Fiber 1g, **Sugars 9g,** Protein 2g, Calcium 2%, Iron 2%. NATURE'S CHOICE/Barbara's Bakery.

The EPIC™ bar—my all-time favorite treat! Compare to a Snickers® Bar:

SUNSPIRE®EPIC™ CHOCOLATE DRENCHED PEANUT CARAMEL. "A Delicious Natural Blast" Sweetened with rice syrup and honey. Available at natural foods markets. Net Wt. 1.75 oz. (50g), Serving Size 1 Bar, Calories 200, Fat Calories 110, Total Fat 12g, Saturated Fat 4g, Cholesterol 9mg, Sodium 36mg, Total Carbohydrate 21g, Fiber 1g, **Sugars 8g,** Protein 5g, Vitamin A 8%, Calcium 4%, Iron 4%. SUNSPIRE® Truly Inspired Natural Candy.™

Even though the following bar is flavored with French Roast espresso beans, I have had no negative caffeine reaction to them. Try them, they're unbelievable.

BARBARA'S NATURE'S CHOICE® 100% NATURAL ESPRESSO BEAN CHOCOLATEY DIPPED DESSERTS. Sweetened with agave nectar, barley malt extract, evaporated cane juice, brown rice syrup. Net Wt. 6.35 oz. (180g), Serving Size 1 bar (30g), Servings 6, Calories 120, Calories from Fat 25, Total Fat 3g, Saturated Fat 2.5g, Cholesterol 0mg, Sodium 10mg, Total Carbohydrate 22g, Dietary Fiber 1g, **Sugars 9g,** Protein 2g, Calcium 2%, Iron 2%. NATURE'S CHOICE® Barbara's Bakery®.

HEALTH VALLEY® STRAWBERRY COBBLER CEREAL BARS. Low Fat. Low Sodium. No Hydrogenated Oils. Certified Organic Flour. No pesticides or chemicals. Good Source of 6 B-Vitamins. Contains Vitamin E & Selenium. No artificial colors, flavors, or preservatives. Sweetened with cane juice, strawberries, dried apples, concentrated fruit juices. Net Wt. 7.9 oz. (224g), Serving Size 1 bar, Servings 6, Calories 130, Calories from Fat 20, Total Fat 2g, Saturated Fat 0g, Cholesterol 0mg, Sodium 50mg, Total Carbohydrate 27g, Dietary Fiber 1g, **Sugars 13g,** Protein 2g, Vitamin 2%, Vitamin E 100%, Riboflavin 10%, Vitamin B_6 10%, Vitamin B_{12} 10%, Iron 4%, Thiamin 10%, Niacin 10%, Folate 10%, Selenium 50%. HEALTH VALLEY COMPANY.

CLIF BAR®
Many other flavors including Cranberry apple cherry, Apricot, Chocolate chip, Chocolate brownie, Chocolate chip peanut crunch, Chocolate almond fudge, Gingersnap, Crunchy peanut butter, and Carrot cake. *Nutrition for sustained energy. Non-GMO soy protein. 23 vitamins &*

minerals. *"Here's the energy you need for the long haul . . . has been shown to help sustain energy levels without a sugar crash." Whole grains and fruit. Wheat and Dairy free. 100% Natural.* Sweetened with brown rice syrup, evaporated cane juice, malt extract, apple fiber, fig paste. COOKIES 'N CREAM. Net Wt. 2.4 oz. (68g), Serving size 1 bar, Calories 230, Calories from Fat 30, Total Fat 3.5g, Saturated Fat 1.5g, Cholesterol 0mg, Sodium 180mg, Potassium 210mg, Total Carbohydrate 39g, Dietary Fiber 5g, **Sugars 21g**, Other Carbohydrate 11g, Protein 10g, Vitamin A 30%, Vitamin C 100%, Calcium 30%, Iron 30%, Vitamin E 100%, Vitamin K 20%, Thiamin (B_1) 25%, Riboflavin (B_2) 15%, Niacin (B_3) 15%, Vitamin B_6 20%, Folate 20%, Vitamin B_{12} 15%, Biotin 15%, Pantothenic Acid 20%, Phosphorus 25%, Iodine 15%, Magnesium 25%, Zinc 20%, Selenium 20%, Copper 25%, Manganese 30%, Chromium 20%, Molybdemum 15%. CLIF BAR, INC.

LUNA™ BAR.
Available in eight other flavors including S'mores, Nuts Over Chocolate, Lemon Zest, Tropical Crisp, Chai Tea, Toasted Nuts 'n Cranberry, and Sesame Raisin Crunch. *A whole nutrition bar created especially for women. Voted Best New Product of 1999 by the food industry. ". . . cross between a Rice Crispies Treat and a chewy granola bar," Cooking Light Magazine Jan/Feb 2000. ". . . the Luna can also double as a multivita-min," Good Housekeeping December 1999. Contains calcium, protein, antioxidants, folic acid, minerals, and soy. Wheat and Dairy Free. Made with non-GMO soy.* Sweetened with brown rice syrup and evaporated cane juice. CHOCOLATE PECAN PIE. Net Wt. 1 Bar (48g), Calories 180, Calories from fat 40, Total Fat 4.5g, Saturated Fat 3g, Polyunsaturated Fat 0.5g, Monounsaturated Fat 1g, Cholesterol 0mg, Sodium 125mg, Potassium 105mg, Total Carbohydrates 24g, Dietary Fiber 2g, **Sugars 12g**, Other Carbohydrates 10g, Protein 10g, Vitamin A 25%, Vitamin C 100%, Calcium 35%, Iron 35%, Vitamin E 100%, Vitamin K 100%, Thiamin (B_1) 100%, Riboflavin (B_2) 100%, Niacin (B_3) 100%, Vitamin B_6 100%, Vitamin B_{12} 100%, Biotin 100%, Pantothenic Acid 100%, Phosphorus 35%, Iodine 35%, Zinc 35%, Selenium 35%, Magnesium 35%, Copper 35%, Manganese 35%, Chromium 35%, Molybdenum 35%. CLIF BAR, INC. *A portion of the proceeds generated by sales of this bar are donated to The Breast Cancer Fund.* ™

Chapter 6
Candy

S ome of the products listed contain "Sugar Alcohol." This is a term that the FDA requires to be used in the Nutrition Facts panel to list a group of artificial sweeteners that are called "Polyols" (See Chapter 1). These include Maltitol and Isomalt. These sweeteners do not contain sugar or alcohol. However, if eaten in excess they may cause a laxative effect due to their slow rate of absorption. Sugar Alcohols do not promote tooth decay. (See also Cookies, Bars, and Chocolate.)

Candy Bars & Chocolate Covered Treats

The EPIC™ bar—my all-time favorite treat! You won't believe it's good for you. Compare to a Snickers® Bar:

SUNSPIRE® EPIC™ CHOCOLATE DRENCHED PEANUT CARAMEL. *"A Delicious Natural Blast"* Available at natural foods markets. Sweetened with Rice Syrup and Honey. Net Wt. 1.75 oz. (50g), Serving Size 1 Bar, Calories 200, Fat Calories 110, Total Fat 12g, Saturated Fat 4g, Cholesterol 9mg, Sodium 36mg, Total Carbohydrate 21g, Fiber 1g, **Sugars 8g,** Protein 5g, Vitamin A 8%, Calcium 4%, Iron 4%. SUNSPIRE® Truly Inspired Natural Candy™

Compare to Almond Joy® Candy Bar:

GLENNY'S COCONUT ALMONDINE. 100% Natural. Moist and Chewy. High in Fiber. High in Iron. No Cholesterol. Available at natural foods markets. Ingredients: *(The ingredients are so great I have to list them all.)* Unsweetened coconut, unsulphured raisins, unsulphured dates, Organic Malt Syrup (Organically grown Corn, Barley, and Brown Rice), Almonds, Brown Rice, and Natural Flavors. Net Wt. 1.5 oz. (42g), Serving Size 1 Bar, Calories 200, Fat Calories 90, Total

Fat 10g, Saturated 7Fat 2g, Cholesterol 0mg, Sodium 20mg, Total Carbohydrate 23g, Dietary Fiber 5g, **Sugars 13g**, Protein 3g, Calcium 2%, Iron 6%. / Distributed By GLENN FOODS, INC.

Compare to Turtles® Boxed Candy:

RUSSELL STOVER® PECAN DELIGHTS.
Sugar-Free. *Pecans and Caramel Covered with a Milk Chocolatey Coating. No Cholesterol.* Sweetened with Maltitol Syrup, Maltitol, Polydextrose. Available at your local pharmacy or confectioner. Net Wt. 3.5 oz. (99g), Serving Size 2 pieces (33g), Servings 3, Calories 170, Calories from Fat 100, Total Fat 12g, Saturated Fat 2.5g, Cholesterol 0mg, Sodium 30mg, Total Carbohydrate 17g, **Sugars 0g**, Maltitol 10g, Protein 2g, Iron 4%. RUSSELL STOVER CANDIES, INC. *"Diabetics: This product may be useful in your diet on the advice of a physician. Not a reduced calorie food. Excessive consumption may cause a laxative effect."*

Compare to Reese's® Peanut Butter Cups:

RUSSELL STOVER® PEANUT BUTTER CUPS.
Sugar-Free Peanut Butter Cups Covered with a Milk Chocolatey Coating. No Cholesterol. Sweetened with Maltitol. Net Wt. 3.5 oz. (99g), Serving Size 4 pieces (36g), Servings 3, Calories 200, Calories from Fat 120, Total Fat 13g, Saturated Fat 6g, Cholesterol 0mg, Sodium 140mg, Total Carbohydrate 17g, **Sugars 0g**, Maltitol 14g, Dietary Fiber 2g, Protein 5g, Iron 2%. RUSSELL STOVER CANDIES, INC. *"Diabetics: This product may be useful in your diet on the advice of a physician. Not a reduced calorie food. Excessive consumption may cause a laxative effect."*

I used to buy the refined sugar version of these chocolate covered wafers. My addiction was so severe that I would unwrap them in the store parking lot, hoping to eat just a couple, but end up eating the whole box (about 40 wafers!) right there in my car. These taste even better than the real thing, result in no guilt, and you can be satisfied with just a couple. I love 'em:

SWEET'N LOW® SUGAR-FREE BRAND CHOCOLATEY WAFER BARS Individually wrapped. 40% Fewer Calories. *"45% Less Fat than the average of the leading chocolate candy brands."* Sweetened with Lactitol, Isomalt, Polydextrose. Available at your local pharmacy or confectioners. Net Wt. 2.75 oz. (78g), Serving Size 3 Bars (47g), Servings 2, Calories 140, Calories from Fat 60, Total Fat 7g, Saturated Fat 6g, Cholesterol 0mg, Sodium 100mg, Total Carbohydrate 23g, Dietary Fiber 1g, **Sugars 0g**, Sugar Alcohol 11g, Protein 4g, Calcium 2%, Iron 2%. *"Benefat™, also known as 'salatrim', is a real fat made from vegetable oil and other components normally found in the diet. It has all the* taste, texture and mouthfeel of traditional fats, but with 45% fewer calories. Only 55% of Benefat™ is absorbed by the body as fat." SIMPLY LITE® FOODS CORP.

Here's the Peanut Butter version. Compare to Reese's®:

SWEET'N LOW® PEANUT BUTTER WAFER BARS.
Sugar-Free. *40% Less Fat. 30% Fewer Calories than the leading Peanut Butter Wafer Bar. Naturally & Artificially Flavored.* Sweetened with Lactitol, Isomalt, and Polydextrose. Net Wt. 2.75 oz. (78g), Serving Size 3 Bars (47g), Servings 2, Calories 160, Fat Calories 80, Total Fat 9g, Polyunsaturated Fat 0g, Monounsaturated Fat 2g, Cholesterol 0mg, Sodium 125mg, Total Carbohydrate 21g, Dietary Fiber 1g, **Sugars 0g,** Sugar Alcohol 9g, Protein 6g, Calcium 2%, Iron 2%. *Contains "Isomalt,® a sugar-free sweetener made from real sugar. It has a pure sweet taste, no unpleasant aftertaste, and only 1/2 the calories of sugar." Contains "Benefat™, also known as 'salatrim', is a real fat made from vegetable oil and other components normally found in the diet. It has all the taste, texture, and mouthfeel of traditional fats, but with 45% fewer calories. Only 55% of Benefat™ is absorbed by the body as fat."* SIMPLY LITE® FOODS.

Compare to York® Peppermint Patties:

SWEET'N LOW® Sugar-Free Brand MINT PATTEEZ™·
Individually wrapped. 45% Fewer Calories. 75% Less Fat than the average of the leading chocolate candy brands. Net Wt. 2.75 oz. (78g), Serving Size 4 pieces (39g), Servings 2, Calories 100, Calories from Fat 20, Total Fat 2g, Saturated Fat 2g, Cholesterol 0mg, Sodium 25mg, Total Carbohydrate 29g, Dietary Fiber 0g, **Sugars 0g**, Sugar Alcohol 24g, Protein 1g. Sweetened with Maltitol, Lactitol, Xylitol, Polydextrose. *Contains "Benefat™ also known as 'salatrim', is a real fat made from vegetable oil and other components normally found in the diet. It has all the taste, texture, and mouthfeel of traditional fats, but with 45% fewer calories. Only 55% of Benefat™ is absorbed by the body as fat."* SIMPLY LITE® FOODS CORP.

RUSSELL STOVER® CARAMELS.
Sugar-Free. *Caramels Covered with a Milk Chocolatey Coating.* Available at your local pharmacy or confectioner. Sweetened with Maltitol and Polydextrose. Net Wt. 3.5 oz. (99g), Serving Size 4 pieces (36g), Servings 3, Calories 170, Calories from Fat 90, Total Fat 10g, Saturated Fat 7g, Cholesterol 5mg, Sodium 5mg, Total Carbohydrate 21g, **Sugars 0g**, Maltitol 20g, Protein 2g. *"Diabetics: This product may be useful in your diet on the advice of a physician. Not a reduced calorie food. Excessive consumption may cause a laxative effect."* RUSSELL STOVER CANDIES, INC.

RUSSELL STOVER® TRUFFLES.
Sugar-Free.*Truffles Covered with a Milk Chocolatey Coating,* Sweetened with Maltitol. Net Wt. 3.5 oz. (99g), Serving Size 4 pieces (36g), Servings 3, Calories 200, Calories from Fat 100, Total Fat 11g, Saturated Fat 7g, Cholesterol 5mg, Sodium 10mg, Total Carbohydrate 24g, **Sugars 0g**, Maltitol 22g, Protein 2g, Iron 2%. *Diabetics: This product may be useful in your diet on the advice of a physician. Not a reduced calorie food. Excessive consumption may cause a laxative effect."* RUSSELL STOVER CANDIES, INC.

Hard Candies

VIVIL® HI-LITES® VITAMIN C SUGAR-FREE HARD CANDIES.
25% Less Calories than regular hard candy. Sweetened with Maltitol Syrup and Fruit Juice. NATURAL WILD BERRY FLAVOR (other flavors available). Net Wt. 2.65 oz. (75g), Serving Size 5 candies (15g), Servings 5, Calories 45, Total Fat 0g, Cholesterol 0mg, Sodium 0mg, Total Carbohydrate 15g, **Sugars 0g**, Maltitol 15g, Protein 0g, Vitamin C 100%. Made in Germany. Manufactured by: VIVIL A. MULLER GMBH & CO. KG for VIVIL AM INC. Distributed by: TROLLI, INC.

BOB'S® BUTTERSCOTCH.
Sugar-Free, Fat-Free, 25% Fewer Calories than regular candy. Sweetened with Aspartame. Available at your local pharmacy. Net Wt. 3 oz. (85g), Serving Size 3 pieces (15g), Servings 6, Calories 45, Total Fat 0g, Sodium 50mg, Total Carbohydrate 15g, **Sugars 0g,** Hydrogenated Starch Hydrolysate 15g, Protein 0g. Product of Mexico. Manufactured for: BOB'S CANDIES, Inc.

LIFESAVERS® DELITES® BUTTER TOFFEE HARD CANDY.
Sugar-Free. 25% Fewer Calories than the leading Butter Toffee Brand. Naturally & Artificially Flavored. Sweetened with Isomalt, Hydrogenated Glucose Syrup. Available at your local pharmacy. Net Wt. 2.75 oz. (78g), Serving Size 5 Candies (15g), Servings 5, Calories 45, Fat Calories 15, Total Fat 2g, Saturated Fat 1g, Cholesterol 5mg, Sodium 95mg, Total Carbohydrate 12g, **Sugars 0g,** Sugar Alcohol 11g. NABISCO, INC.

LIFESAVERS® DELITES® ORCHARD FRUITS HARD CANDY.
Sugar-Free. 50% Fewer Calories than the leading Hard Candy Brands. Naturally & Artificially Flavored. Sweetened with Isomalt, Hydrogenated Glucose Syrup. CHERRY, GREEN APPLE, RED RASPBERRY, PEACH. Net Wt. 2.75 oz. (78g), Serving Size 5 Candies (15g), Servings 5, Calories 30, Fat Calories 0, Total Fat 0g, Saturated Fat 0g, Cholesterol 0mg, Sodium 0mg, Total Carbohydrate 15g, **Sugars 0g,** Sugar Alcohol 14g. NABISCO.

SWEET'N LOW® SUGAR-FREE BRAND FRUIT FLAVORS HARD CANDY. *Individually wrapped. 50% Fewer Calories than sugar hard candy. Sweetened with "Isomalt,® a sugar-free sweetener made from real sugar.* Net Wt. 2.75 oz. (78g), Serving Size 5 pieces (15g), Servings 5, Calories 30, Calories from Fat 0, Total Fat 0g, Saturated Fat 0g, Cholesterol 0mg, Sodium 0mg, Total Carbohydrate 15g, Dietary Fiber 0g, **Sugars 0g**, Protein 0g. *It has a pure sweet taste, no unpleasant aftertaste, and only 1/2 the calories of sugar. Contains "Benefat,™ also known as 'salatrim', is a real fat made from vegetable oil and other components normally found in the diet. It has all the taste, texture and mouthfeel of traditional fats, but with 45% fewer calories. Only 55% of Benefat™ is absorbed by the body as fat."* SIMPLY LITE® FOODS CORP.

ECKERD AWARD SUGAR-FREE, FAT-FREE, HARD CANDIES. *"An Orchard of Flavors–Assorted Fruits" Artificially Flavored. 33% Fewer Calories Than Regular Hard Candy.* Sweetened with Isomalt and Aspartame. Net Wt. 4 oz. (113g), Serving Size 4 pieces, Servings 6, Calories 45, Total Fat 0g, Sodium 0mg, Total Carbohydrate 17g, **Sugars 0g**, Sugar Alcohol 17g, Protein 0g. ECKERD DRUG COMPANY.

Chewy Candies

Compare to Tootsie Rolls® Brand:

GO LIGHTLY® SUGAR-FREE FUDGIE ROLLS. *Artificially-flavored chewy chocolate candy.* Sweetened with Aspartame. Net Wt. 3.5 oz. (99g), Serving Size 6 pieces (38g), Servings 2.5, Calories 130, Fat Calories 45, Total Fat 5g, Saturated Fat 2g, Cholesterol 5mg, Sodium 25mg, Total Carbohydrate 28g, **Sugars 0g**, Hydrogenated Starch Hydrolysate 28g, Protein 1g. GOLIGHTLY CANDY CO., INC.

Compare to the Gummy Bears® Brand. I thought I'd never be able to eat these kinds of treats again. But, thanks to Hain Pure Foods Kidz,™ I can have these candies without harmful side-effects. Your children won't know the difference. Games and special offers on the back panel:

HAIN PURE FOODS KIDZ™ BEAR BITES™ GUMMY FRUIT SNACKS. *All Natural. No Artificial Flavor. 100% Vitamin C Per Serving. No Preservatives. Fat Free.* Sweetened with evaporated cane juice, grape juice concentrate, natural extract of corn and barley malt. Net Wt. 3.75 oz. (106g), 5–0.75 oz. (21g) Pouches, Serving Size 9 pieces (21g), Servings per container 5, Calories 60, Fat Calories 0, Total Fat 0, Saturated Fat 0g, Cholesterol 0mg, Sodium

15mg, Total Carbohydrate 14g, **Sugars 13g**, Protein 2g, Vitamin C 100%. Manufactured for Distribution by: THE HAIN FOOD GROUP, INC.

GO LIGHTLY® SUGAR-FREE ASSORTED TOFFEES.

Reduced Calorie, 25% Less Calories than regular Toffees. Imported from France. Low Fat. Sweetened with Maltitol, Mannitol, and Aspartame. Net Wt. 3.5 oz. (99g), Serving Size 7 pieces (40g), Servings 2.5, Calories 120, Fat Calories 15, Total Fat 1.5g, Saturated Fat 0g, Cholesterol 0mg, Sodium 0mg, Total Carbohydrate 35g, **Sugars 0g,** Sugar Alcohols 35g, Protein 1g. GOLIGHTLY CANDY CO., INC.

FRUIT SOFTEES™ MACADAMIA NUT CANDIES.

Sugar-Free. *Low-fat tropical fruits. No cholesterol. Low sodium. No preservatives. Natural & Artificial Flavors.* Sweetened with Maltitol Syrup, Sorbitol, Maltitol. Four Flavors: *PINEAPPLE, BANANA, COCONUT, PASSION-ORANGE.* Net Wt. 3.65 oz. (104g), Serving Size 3 pieces (35g), Servings 3, Calories 140, Fat Calories 25, Total Fat 3g, Saturated Fat .5g, Sodium 35mg, Total Carbohydate 27g, **Sugars 0g,** Sugar Alcohols 11g, Protein 1g. *"If you are diabetic, this product may be useful in your diet on the advice of a physician. This not a reduced calorie food. This product cannot be used to counteract an insulin reaction."* LIBERTY ORCHARDS CO. INC.

FRUIT SOFTEES™ SUGAR-FREE FRUIT & NUT CANDIES.

Low Fat Orchard Fruits. No Cholesterol. Low Sodium. No Preservatives. Natural & Artificial Flavors. Sweetened with Maltitol Syrup, Sorbitol, Maltitol. Delicious Flavors: CHERRY-PECAN, BOYSENBERRY-PECAN, STRAWBERRY-WALNUT, RASPBERRY-PECAN, APPLE-WALNUT, ORANGE-WALNUT. Net Wt. 3.65 oz. (104g), Serving Size 3 pieces (35g), Servings 3, Calories 140, Fat Calories 25, Total Fat 3g, Sodium 35mg, Total Carbohydate 27g, **Sugars 0g,** Sugar Alcohols 11g, Protein 1g. *"If you are diabetic, this product may be useful in your diet on the advice of a physician. This not a reduced calorie food. This product cannot be used to counteract an insulin reaction."* LIBERTY ORCHARDS CO., INC.

SORBEE® FRUGELI™ SUGAR-FREE FRUIT FLAVORED JELLY CANDY. *30% Less Calories than Sugar Jelly Candy. No Sugar. No Saccharin. No Aftertaste. No Preservatives. Fat Free. Cholesterol Free. No MSG.* Sweetened with Maltitol Syrup, Isomalt, and Aspartame. Artificial Flavors: *CHERRY, LEMON, RASPBERRY, PEACH, STRAWBERRY, MELON.* Net Wt. 4 oz. (113g), Serving Size 4 pieces, Servings 2.5, Calories 90, Total Fat 0g, Saturated Fat 0g, Cholesterol 0mg, Sodium 50mg, Total Carbohydrate 34g, **Sugars 0g,** Sugar Alcohols 34g. Imported by: SORBEE INTERNATIONAL LIMITED.

Molasses is high in iron and better than refined sugar but it is still a sugar and should be limited. If you love licorice, choose this bar over regular brands for the all-natural alternative:

PANDA® LICORICE BAR, The Real Taste of Licorice®
All-natural ingredients. Sweetened with Molasses. Available at natural foods markets. Net Wt. 1 1/8 oz. (32g), Serving Size 1 Bar (32g), Calories 110, Fat Calories 0, Total Fat 0g, Saturated Fat 0g, Cholesterol 0mg, Sodium 65mg, Total Carbohydrate 25g, **Sugars 16g**, Protein 1g, Calcium 4%, Iron 9%. . Imported to the USA by: NEW WORLD MARKETING GROUP, LLC/Manufactured by OY PANDA AB, Finland.

This brand of licorice is sugar-free:

REDVINES® BRAND LICORICE TWISTS
Sugar-free, fat-free. Quality since 1914. Low Sodium. Sweetened with Maltitol Syrup. Available at your local pharmacy. Flavors: STRAWBERRY AND REGULAR. Net Wt. 6 oz. (170g), Serving Size 6 Twists (40g), Servings 4, Calories 140, Fat Calories 0, Total Fat 0g, Sodium 5mg, Total Carbohydrate 32g, **Sugars 0g,** Maltitol 14g, Protein 1g. AMERICAN LICORICE CO.

Chapter 7
Cereals

Ordinary breakfast cereal (the kind we grew up with and the kind that some people still feed their children) contains as much sugar per serving as a can of soda pop; as much as five to ten teaspoons per bowl! And that's before any added fruit or spooned on additions from the sugar jar.

Check your label. I consider cereals with three to seven grams of added sugar as low sugar, but it is still important to watch your number of servings. Read the side panel for exact serving size. Consider twelve to twenty grams of sugar per meal the maximum, and, of course, tolerances will vary.

Add to unsweetened cereals: fruit (bananas, berries, raisins), a small amount of honey or molasses (half a teaspoon), or a brand name artificial or natural sweetener (See Chapter 1). Be sure to include this in your overall sugar count. But like my husband and I, you may even develop a taste for cereals *as is*. For added nutrition you can include a sprinkling of almonds, soy nuts, sunflower seeds, or pumpkin seeds. Unless you are following food-combining guidelines (no starch and protein together), you may want to add a scoop of protein powder as well. Add it all up; the correct protein to carbohydrate ratio being somewhere around 15 grams of protein to 20 grams of carbohydrate. Read Dr. Barry Sears *The Zone* to determine your own ideal figures based on body size and level of activity.

Cereals

YOGI BHAJAN'S PEACE CEREALS®.
All Natural. Organically Grown. Sweetened with Unsulphured Molasses, Honey, Evaporated Cane Juice. Flavors include: VANILLA ALMOND CRISP, MAPLE RAISIN CRISP, RASPBERRY SUGAR CRISP, CINNAMON APPLE CRISP, MANGO PASSION CRISP, WILD BERRY CRISP. Net Wt. 115 oz., Serving Size 1

cup, Servings 5, Calories 220, Fat Calories 50, Saturated Fat .5g, Cholesterol 0mg, Sodium 200mg, Carbohydrate 38g, **Sugars 10g**, Protein 5g, Calcium 2%, Iron 6%. GOLDEN TEMPLE.

BARBARA'S PUFFINS®.
95% Fat-free, Sweetened with Unsulphured Molasses. Net Wt. 12 oz., Serving Size 3/4 cup, Servings 11, Calories 100, Fat Calories 10, Total Fat 1g, Cholesterol 0mg, Carbohydrate 26g, Fiber 6g, **Sugars 6g**, Protein 2g, Sodium 6%, Potassium 2%, Vitamin C 15%, Iron 1%, Vitamin E 2%. BARBARA'S BAKERY.

KOUNTRY FRESH® TOASTED OATS.
Meets the U. S. Government requirements for low-fat, low-saturated fat, low-cholesterol food. Good Source of 13 vitamins & minerals including calcium. Sweetened with Sugar. Net Wt. 15 oz. (425g), Serving size 1 cup (30g), Servings per container 14, Calories 110, Calories from Fat 15, Total Fat 1.5g, Saturated Fat 0g, Cholesterol 0mg, Sodium 240mg, Potassium 90mg, Total Carbohydrate 22g, Dietary Fiber 3g, **Sugars 1g**, Protein 4g. Plus 15 vitamins and minerals. ASTOR PRODUCTS.

GENERAL MILLS WHOLE GRAIN TOTAL®.
Whole Grain Wheat & Brown Rice Flakes, Sweetened with Sugar. Net Wt. 12 oz. (340g), Serving size 3/4 cup (30g), Servings per container 11, Calories 110, Calories from Fat 10, Total Fat 1g, Saturated Fat 0.5g, Cholesterol 0mg, Sodium 200mg, Potassium 100mg, Total Carbohydrate 24g, Dietary Fiber 3g, **Sugars 5g**, Other Carbohydrate 16g, Protein 3g, Vitamin A 10%, Vitamin C 25%, Calcium 25% (with milk 40%), Iron 100%, Vitamin D 10%, Vitamin E 100%, Thiamin 100%, Riboflavin 100%, Niacin 100%, Vitamin B_6 100%, Folic Acid 100%, Vitamin B_{12} 100%, Pantothenic Acid 100%, Phosphorus 8%, Magnesium 6%, Zinc 100%, Copper 4%. GENERAL MILLS SALES.

GREAT VALUE™ CRUNCHY NUGGETS CEREAL.
Unsweetened. Net Wt. 24 oz. (1lb 8oz) 680g, Serving size 1/2 cup (48g), Servings per container 14, Calories 170, Calories from Fat 10, Total Fat 1g, Saturated Fat 0g, Cholesterol 0mg, Sodium 210mg, Potassium 190mg, Total Carbohydrate 38g, Dietary Fiber 5g, **Sugars 3g**, Other Carbohydrate 30g, Protein 6g, Vitamin A 25%, Iron 80%, Vitamin D 10%, Thiamine 25%, Riboflavin 25%, Niacin 25%, Vitamin B_6 25%, Folate 25%, Vitamin B_{12} 25%, Phosphorous 15%, Magnesium 10%, Zinc 15%, Copper 10%. Marketed by: WALMART® Stores, Inc.

GREAT VALUE™ HEALTHY 4 YOU ENRICHED BRAN FLAKES.
Cereal with 12 vitamins and minerals. Low-Fat. Cholesterol-Free. High Iron. Good source of high fiber. Sweetened with Sugar and Corn Syrup. Net Wt. 17.3 oz. (1 lb 1.3oz) 490g, Serving size 3/4 cup (31g), Servings per container 16, Calories 110, Calories from Fat 5, Total Fat 0.5g, Saturated Fat 0g, Cholesterol 0mg, Sodium 220mg, Total Carbohydrate 25g, Dietary Fiber 5g, **Sugars 5g**, Other Carbohydrate 15g, Protein 3g, Vitamin A 25% (10% as Beta Carotene), Vitamin C 25%, Iron 50%, Vitamin D 10%, Vitamin E 25%, Thiamine 25%, Riboflavin 25%, Niacin 25%,

Vitamin B_6 25%, Folate 25%, Vitamin B_{12} 25%, Phosphorus 15%, Magnesium 10%, Zinc 25%, Copper 8%. WALMART® Stores, Inc.

GREAT VALUE™ MULTI-GRAIN FLAKES CEREAL.
Sweetened with Sugar and Corn syrup. Ingredients include whole wheat flour, wheat bran, de-germed yellow corn meal, rolled oats, and brown rice flour. Net Wt. 17.3 oz. (1 lb. 1.3oz) 490g. Serving size 3/4 cup (30g), Servings per container 16, Calories with skim milk 160, Calories from fat 10, Total Fat 1g, Saturated Fat 0g, Cholesterol 0mg, Sodium 170mg, Total Carbohydrate 24g, Dietary Fiber 3g, **Sugars 5g,** Protein 3g. Percent Daily Values with skim milk: Vitamin A 30%, Vitamin C 25%, Calcium 15%, Iron 50%, Vitamin D 25%, Vitamin E 25%, Thiamin 30%, Riboflavin 35%, Niacin 25%, Vitamin B_6 25%, Folate 25%, Vitamin B_{12} 35%, Zinc 30%. WALMART® Stores, Inc.

Our family favorite!:

POST HONEY BUNCHES OF OATS® CEREAL WITH ALMONDS.
Toasted Corn & Wheat Flakes with Crunchy Oat Clusters & Almonds. Provides 9 essential vitamins and minerals. Sweetened with Sugar, Brown Sugar, Barley Syrup, and Honey. Available at most grocery stores. Net Wt. 16 oz. (1 lb.) (453g), Serving Size 3/4 cup (31g), Servings per container 15, Calories 130, Calories from Fat 25, Total Fat 2.5g, Saturated Fat 0.5g, Cholesterol 0mg, Sodium 190mg, Potassium 60mg, Total Carbohydrate 24g, Dietary Fiber 1g, **Sugars 6g,** Other Carbohydrate 17g, Protein 3g, Vitamin A 15%, Iron 45%, Vitamin D 10%, Thiamin 25%, Riboflavin 25%, Niacin 25%, Vitamin B_6 25%, Folic Acid 25%, Vitamin B_{12} 25%, Phosphorus 6%, Zinc 2%, Copper 4%. KRAFT FOODS.

PUFFED KASHI® SEVEN WHOLE GRAINS & SESAME.
Received the Veri-Pure™ Seal of Approval for no pesticide residue. Unsweetened. Available at health food and grocery stores. Net Wt 7.5 oz (212.6g), Serving size 1 cup (25g), Servings per container 8.5, Calories 70, Calories from fat 5, Total Fat 1g, Saturated Fat 0g, Total Carbohydrate 13g, Dietary Fiber 2g, **Sugars 0g,** Protein 3, Thiamin 2% DV, Niacin 4% DV, Potassium 2% DV, Iron 4% DV, Riboflavin 2% DV, Phosphorus 6% DV. KASHI CO.

UNCLE SAM® CEREAL.
Toasted Whole-Grain Wheat Flakes with Crispy Whole Flaxseed. *All-natural. Low Sodium. Contains Flaxseed–2000 mg Omega-3 Fatty Acids per Serving. No Artificial Colors. No Preservatives.* Sweetened with Barley Malt. Net Wt. 10 oz. (284g), Serving Size 1 Cup (55g), Servings 5, Calories 190, Fat Calories 40, Total Fat 5g, Saturated Fat 0.5g, Cholesterol 0mg, Sodium 135mg, Total Carbohydrate 38g, Dietary Fiber 10g, **Sugars 1g,** Protein 7g, Vitamin C, 2%, Calcium 4%, Iron 10%, Thiamin 50%, Riboflavin 50%, Niacin 50%. U.S. MILLS, INC.

Natural and Sugar Free Sweeteners
(See Chapter 1.)

Chapter 8
Chocolate

Yes, chocolate deserves a chapter all its own. Who can live without chocolate? The good news is that you can have your chocolate and eat it too! Women, our monthly craving for chocolate to boost our serotonin level can be satisfied without ill effects by eating fructose sweetened chocolate found in the diet or dietetic section of almost any supermarket. There are great choices at the health food store too. But be sure to look for "sucrose free." Know that not everything in the health food store is healthy. Always choose sugar-free or the less refined options.

Most of these stores have "carob clusters", which are wonderful alternatives to regular chocolate. Found in the store's bulk bins are also peanut clusters, caramel nut clusters, coconut clusters (my favorite), raisin nut clusters, carob and yogurt covered nuts.

Of course, almost all these alternatives are high in fat. They should be limited only to those times of special craving. Fortunately, without a great deal of added white sugar, it is easier to eat less of these products. You can satisfy your craving and be done with it. You will soon be enjoying your chocolate without any feeling of guilt. There is nothing in the world like a guilt-free chocolate bar, and the flavors are all the ones you love: rice crisp, almond, fruit & nut, mint, and even caramel pecan. If the grocery store and health food market chocolates are not satisfying enough, almost every gourmet chocolate shop has a sugar-free section with choices like raspberry truffles, orange cream meltaways, almond fudge, chocolate coconut clusters, and even more exotic flavors like cappuccino cream. (See also Chapter 5: Bars.)

Note: Be conscious of the serving size and amount of sugar grams. The same rules apply. Try to avoid having more than about twelve grams of sugar per sitting, and try to eat all snacks (even low sugar or natural sugar ones) with a meal. Yes, I did say have your dessert! Remember, if you eat carbohydrates without enough protein to balance your metabolism, you will block fat stores from being burned as energy. The result? More and more weight retention. So, eat your dessert and try to eat at least every four to five hours—but with no snacking in between. You'll be amazed at the results. One more thing. Should you have a weak moment and grab a snack in between—so what, it's low sugar, right? Enjoy!

Chocolate Choices

The EPIC™ bar–My all-time favorite treat! Compare to a Snick-ers® Bar:

SUNSPIRE® EPIC™ CHOCOLATE DRENCHED PEANUT CARAMEL. *"A Delicious Natural Blast,"* Sweetened with Rice Syrup and Honey. Available at most health food markets. Net Wt. 1.75 oz. (50g), Serving Size 1 Bar, Calories 200, Fat Calories 110, Total Fat 12g, Saturated Fat 4g, Cholesterol 9mg, Sodium 36mg, Total Carbohydrate 21g, Fiber 1g, **Sugars 8g,** Protein 5g, Vitamin A 8%, Calcium 4%, Iron 4%. SUNSPIRE® Truly Inspired Natural Candy™

Our favorite theater snack!

CLOUD NINE® CHOCOLATE–BUTTER NUT TOFFEE. *Only pure and natural ingredients. Cane juice sweetened. 10% of profits are donated to conserve tropical rainforests.* Sweetened with Evaporated Cane Juice and Corn Syrup. Available at most health food markets. Flavors: ESPRESSO BEAN CRUNCH and PEANUT BUTTER BRITTLE. Net Wt. 3oz. (85g), Serving Size 1/2 Bar, Servings 2, Calories 230, Calories from Fat 130, Total Fat 14g, Saturated Fat 8g, Cholesterol 5mg, Sodium 30mg, Total Carbohydrate 25g, Fiber 1g, **Sugars 21g**, Protein 3g, Vitamin A 2%, Vitamin C 2%, Calcium 6%, Iron 6%. Distributor: CLOUD NINE, INC.

TROPICAL SOURCE.® CHOCOLATE WILD RICE CRISP. *100% Dairy-Free. Roasted Puffed Wild Rice in Dairy Free Chocolate. 10% of profits to conserve tropical rain forests. No Cholesterol.* Sweetened with Evaporated Cane Juice. Available at most health food markets. Net Wt. 3 oz. (85g), Serving Size 1/2 Bar (43g), Servings 2, Calories 230, Calories from Fat 124, Total Fat 14g, Saturated Fat 8g, Cholesterol 0mg, Sodium 16mg, Total Carbohydrate 26g, Fiber 1g, **Sugars 23g**, Protein 3g. Distributor: CLOUD NINE, INC., USA.

TROPICAL SOURCE® DARK CHOCOLATE, TOASTED ALMOND. *Dairy-Free . No Cholesterol.* Sweetened with Evaporated Cane Juice. Available at most health food markets. Net Wt. 3 oz. (85g), Serving Size 1/2 Bar (43g), Servings 2, Calories 248, Calories from Fat 151, Total Fat 17g, Saturated Fat 8g,

Cholesterol 0mg, Sodium 15mg, Total Carbohydrate 21g, Fiber 1g, **Sugars 19g**, Protein 3g. Distributor: CLOUD NINE, INC. *10% of profits to conserve tropical rain forests.*

ESTEE® MILK CHOCOLATE WITH CRISP RICE.
Sweetened with Fructose.Available at most grocery stores. Other flavors include: Mint, Almonds, and Fruit. Net Wt. 2.3 oz. (65g), Serving size 1 bar, Calories 370, Calories from Fat 230, Total Fat 26g, Saturated Fat 15g, Cholesterol 30mg, Sodium 110mg, Potassium 340 mg, Total Carbohydrate 29g, **Sugars 24g**, Protein 7g. THE HAIN FOOD GROUP, Inc.

Chocolate Alternatives

YOGAFECTION™ BRAZIL NUT CRUNCH.
Date-sweetened yogurt confection contains no refined sugars. Texture of real chocolate. Tastes great. Sweetened with Dates and Barley Malt Powder. Net Wt. 3 oz. (85g), Serving Size 1/3 bar, Servings 3, Calories 190, Fat Calories 110, Total Fat 13g, Saturated Fat 9g, Cholesterol 5mg, Sodium 65mg, Total Carbohydrate 16g, Fiber 0g, **Sugars 13g**, Protein 2g, Iron 2%. AMERICAN NUTRITIONAL SNACKS. *With every purchase American Natural Snacks donates money to groups working to protect the environment.*

CHATFIELD'S CAROB & COMPLIMENTS CAROB POWDER.
A chocolate alternative for smoothies, hot drinks, or baking. No added sugar. Fat-free. Cholesterol-free. No caffeine. No chocolate or Cocoa. No added sweeteners. Net Wt. 16 oz. (1 lb), 454g, Serving size 1/4 cup, Servings per container 15, Calories 60, Fat Calories 0, Total Fat 0g, Saturated Fat 0g, Cholesterol 0mg, Sodium 10mg, Total Carbohydrate 27g, Fiber 3g, **Sugars 16g**, Protein 1g, Calcium 10%, Iron 4%. Distributed by: AMERICAN NATURAL SNACKS.

Chapter 9
Drinks:
Nutrition/Soy/
Chocolate Milk/ Rice/Eggnog.

S oy is an excellent food that has estrogenic qualities. In Nina Anderson and Dr. Howard Peiper's book *The Secrets of Staying Young*, it is noted that soy is most beneficial when taken in *fermented* form, such as foods that include tempeh and miso (See Chapter 18). Sprouted soy is also available in supplement form or as a powder to use in protein drinks. It has no side effects and is easily assimilated by the body. Fermented soy is more digestible than the unfermented soy commonly used in tofu and soy milk. Check your local health foods market for these products.

Soy is especially helpful in reducing the risk of cancer. It contains weak estrogens, referred to as isoflavones that compete with the body's full strength estrogenic hormones in accessing cells. These isoflavones mimic estrogen hormones by binding to cell receptors that would normally attract the body's own estrogen. Because the growth signal of isoflavones is so much weaker than normal estrogen, excess estrogen growth is inhibited.

The soy products listed in this chapter are not produced from fermented soy, but these foods may be a better choice than cow's milk that may contain added growth hormones. They are dairy-free, safe for vegetarian consumption, and are either low in sugar or contain only natural sugars. Hypoglycemics should be cautious with those products that contain more than 12 grams of sugar per serving, albeit natural sugars. Diabetics may want to avoid these items altogether. Alternatives to soy milk include almond milk and rice milk.

Nutrition

BALANCED™ THE TOTAL NUTRITIONAL DRINK.
"Ready To Drink Meal" All Natural. 15 Grams Soy Protein. 30% Daily Value of Protein. Dairy-Free, Lactose-Free. Cholesterol-free. Low Fat. Good source of calcium and fiber. 25 Vitamins and Minerals. Isoflavones. Sweetened with Dehydrated Cane Juice. Available in your health food market. Flavors: VANILLA, STRAWBERRY, CHOCOLATE. Net Wt. 11 fl. oz. (325 ml), Serving size 1 can, Calories 230, Calories from Fat 25, Total Fat 3g, Saturated Fat 0.5g, Cholesterol 0mg, Sodium 220mg, Potassium 360mg, Total Carbohydrate 35g, Dietary Fiber 3g, **Sugars 19g**, Protein 15g., 25 vitamins and minerals 25–50% Daily Values. Distributed by: AMERICAN NATURAL SNACKS.

BIOCHEM® SPORTS & FITNESS SYSTEMS ULTIMATE LO CARB PROTEIN SHAKE. *35 Grams of Protein. Total Nutrition in a Single Serving. Natural and Artificial Flavors.* Sweetened with Sucralose. Available at the health foods market. Net Wt 12 fl. oz. (354 ml), Serving Size 1 Can, Calories 170, Fat Calories 5, Total Fat 0.5g, Saturated Fat 0g, Cholesterol 5mg, Sodium 115mg, Potassium 230mg, Total Carbohydrate 6g, Dietary Fiber 2g, **Sugars 3g**, Protein 35g, Calcium 100%, Riboflavin 10%, Vitamin B12 35%, Phosphorus 70%, Iron 2%, Vitamin B6 4%, Pantotheric Acid 2%, Magnesium 20%. BIOCHEM.

Soy Milk

There are many more soy drinks and soy products available at your natural foods market. These are some of our favorites.

WESTSOY® WESTBRAE NATURAL® LOW FAT SOY DRINK.
Contains calcium & vitamins A & D and 18mg of Isoflavones per serving. Organic. Lactose-free. Nondairy. Cholesterol-free. Sweetened with Malt Cereal Extract. Available at health food stores. VANILLA. 32 fl. oz.   (1 qt.), Serving Size 1 cup, 8 fl. oz. (240ml), Servings about 4, Amount Per Serving: Calories 110, Calories From Fat 15, Total Fat 1.5g, Saturated Fat 0g, Polyunsaturated Fat 1g, Monounsaturated Fat 0.5g, Cholesterol 0mg, Sodium 70mg, Potassium 150mg, Total Carbohydrate 20g, Dietary Fiber 2g, **Sugars 10g**, Protein 4g, Vitamin A 10% D.V., Calcium 20% D.V., Iron 6% D.V., Vitamin D 25% D.V. Manufactured by: THE HAIN FOOD GROUP, INC.

WHITE WAVE SILK™ VANILLA SOY MILK.
Calcium enriched. Low 1% Fat & Vitamin enriched. Certified GMO-free (Genetically Modified Organism) Soy. Sweetened with Naturally Milled Organic Cane. Available at health food and grocery stores. 1 quart (946 ml), Serving Size 1 cup (240 ml), Servings per container 4, Calories 90, Calories from Fat 30, Total Fat 3g, Saturated Fat 0g, Cholesterol 0mg, Sodium 95mg, Total Carbohydrate 10g,

Sugars 6g, Protein 6.5g, Vitamin A 10%, Calcium 30%, Iron 2%, Riboflavin 30%, Vitamin D 30%, Vitamin B_{12} 50%. Distributed by: WHITE WAVE, INC.

Chocolate Milk

WHITE WAVE SILK™ CHOCOLATE SOY MILK.
Calcium enriched. Low 1% Fat & Vitamin enriched. Certified GMO-free (Genetically Modified Organism) Soy. Sweetened with Naturally Milled Organic Cane. Available at health food stores. 1 quart (946 ml), Serving Size 1 cup (240 ml), Servings per container 4, Calories 130, Calories from Fat 20, Total Fat 2.5g, Saturated Fat 0g, Cholesterol 0mg, Sodium 75mg, Total Carbohydrate 23g, **Sugars 19g**, Protein 5g, Vitamin A 10%, Calcium 30%, Iron 2%, Riboflavin 30%, Vitamin D 30%, Vitamin B_{12} 50%. Distributed by: WHITE WAVE, INC.

VITASOY® LIGHT COCOA.
Natural Soy Drink. *18mg Isoflavones per Serving. Made with Whole Organic Soybeans. 1% Fat. Reduced Calories.* Sweetened with Cane Juice and Malt. Available at health food stores. Net Wt. 32 fl. oz. (1 qt) 946ml, Serving Size 8 fl. oz. (240ml), Servings 4, Calories 80, Fat Calories 20, Total Fat 2g, Saturated Fat 1g, Polyunsaturated Fat 1g, Monounsaturated Fat 0.5g, Cholesterol 0mg, Sodium 130mg, Total Carbohydrate 13g, Dietary Fiber 1g, **Sugars 9g**, Other Carbohydrates 3g, Protein 4g, Calcium 6%, Iron 4%. VITASOY USA, INC.

VITASOY® LIGHT CAROB SUPREME.
Natural Soy Drink. *31mg Isoflavones per Serving! Made with Whole Organic Soybeans. Cholesterol-free. Lactose-free. Dairy-free. No Artificial Preservatives, Sweeteners, Colors, or Flavors.* Sweetened with Cane Juice and Malt. Available at health food stores. Net Wt. 32 fl oz. (1 qt) 946ml, Serving Size 8 fl. oz. (240ml), Servings 4, Calories 150, Fat Calories 40, Total Fat 4.5g, Saturated Fat 1g, Polyunsaturated Fat 2.5g, Monounsaturated Fat 1g, Cholesterol 0mg, Sodium 160mg, Total Carbohydrate 22g, Dietary Fiber 1g, **Sugars 9g**, Other Carbohydrates 11g, Protein 7g, Calcium 6%, Iron 4%. VITASOY USA, INC.

BLUE DIAMOND® GROWER'S CO-OP™ ALMOND BREEZE.™
Chocolate Non-Dairy Beverage made from real almonds. No Lactose. Only 1% Fat. Contains Calcium, Vitamins A, D, & E. Cholesterol Free. Sweetened with Evaporated Cane Juice. Available at health food stores. Net Wt. 32 fl. oz. (1 qt.) 946 ml, Serving Size 8 fl. oz. (240 ml), Servings 4, Calories 120, Fat Calories 25, Total Fat 3g, Saturated Fat 0g, Cholesterol 0mg, Sodium 160mg, Potassium 180mg, Total Carbohydrate 21g, Dietary Fiber 1g, **Sugars 20g**, Protein 1g, Vitamin A 10%, Vitamin D 25%, Vitamin E 50%, Iron 4%, Calcium 20%. BLUE DIAMOND GROWERS.

Rice Milk

RICE DREAM® VANILLA RICE MILK.
1% Fat. Non-Dairy Beverage. Lactose Free. Made from California Brown Rice. Soy Free. No Cholesterol. 100% Vegetarian. Low in Sodium. Serve chilled or hot. No Added Sweeteners. Available at health food and grocery stores. Net Wt. 32 fl. oz. (1 qt) 946ml, Serving Size 8 fl. oz. (240ml), Servings 4, Calories 130, Fat Calories 20, Total Fat 2g, Saturated Fat 0g, Cholesterol 0mg, Sodium 90mg, Total Carbohydrate 28g, **Sugars 12g**, Protein 1g, Vitamin E 4%, Calcium 2%. IMAGINE FOODS, INC.

Eggnog

So much better than the real thing. Lighter, less sweet and sticky. No unusual after-taste. During the holidays, we can't get enough:

WHITE WAVE SILK™ EGGNOG.
Naturally-sweetened with evaporated cane juice. Sweetened with Evaporated Cane Juice. Available at health food stores during the holiday season. 1 quart, Serving Size 1/2 cup (120 ml), 8 Servings, Calories 80, Total Fat 1g, Saturated Fat 0g, Cholesterol 0mg, Sodium 75mg, Total Carbohydrate 15g, **Sugars 12g**, Protein 2g, Calcium 2%, Iron 4%. Distributed by WHITE WAVE, INC.

Chapter 10
Hot Drinks

C affeine is the most popular addictive (psychoactive!) drug in the world. It increases the brain's metabolism but reduces blood flow to the brain. Caffeine increases the stimulating neurohormone, noradrenaline, and reduces the calming neurotransmitter, serotonin. It increases excretion of calcium from the bones which contributes to osteoporosis and lowers the blood glucose level in a hypoglycemic while raising it in a diabetic. Caffeine stimulates the adrenal glands prompting the liver to release sugar into the bloodstream, increases blood pressure which adds to heart disease risk, and increases the risk of birth defects. Need I say more?

The effects of coffee with added sugar are doubly severe. A soft drink loaded with sugar, caffeine, sodium, and phosphoric acid is devastating. One caffeinated beverage can have as much as two to three times as much caffeine as an aspirin tablet; up to 150 mg.

Symptoms associated with caffeine consumption include headaches, insomnia, anxiety attacks, heart flutters, thoughts that race uncontrollably, irritability, nervous agitation, trembling, paranoia, night terrors, nightmares, hallucinations, and seizure disorders. If you think you need that morning cup to wake you up, consider the side effects of this *drug*. Be conscious of the fact that caffeine *is* a drug. Treat it with the contempt that it deserves.

On a brighter note, the ritual of having a hot drink at a special time need not be eliminated. There are alternative choices including many assorted and flavorful decaffeinated teas. Decaf coffee is also acceptable but do be aware that *decaffeinated* does not necessarily mean caffeine free. A regular cup of coffee can have anywhere from ten milligrams of caffeine up to one-hundred milligrams depending on the strength; a cup of decaffeinated coffee, usually about four to twelve. It varies greatly. Just as with sugar, reduce slowly to avoid symptoms of withdrawal such as headache and fatigue. These symptoms do pass, but may take anywhere from one to three weeks to do so. Keep in mind that you are experiencing *drug* withdrawal symptoms, (See Chapter 1: Natural Sweeteners for low glycemic sweeteners that you can add to your unsweetened coffees and teas).

Sugar-Free & Caffeine-Free Coffee/ Sugar-Free Coffee Substitutes

POSTUM® INSTANT HOT BEVERAGE NATURAL COFFEE FLAVOR. *Rich, Full-bodied Taste. Naturally Caffeine-free. Made from a special blend of roasted grains including wheat, wheat bran, and natural coffee flavor.* Sweetened with Molasses and Maltodextrin from corn. Net Wt. 4 oz. (113g), Serving Size 1 tsp (3g), makes 8 fl. oz., Servings 38, Calories 10, Total Fat 0g, Sodium 0mg, Total Carbohydrate 3g, Protein 0g. KRAFT FOODS, INC.

GENERAL FOODS INTERNATIONAL COFFEES.®
Sugar-Free, Caffeine-free and Sugar-free, Smooth, creamy, delicious. Also Fat-free. Sweetened with Maltodextrin (from corn), Aspartame, and Acesulfame Potassium. Flavors: SWISS MOCHA, FRENCH VANILLA. Net Wt. 4.4 oz. (124g), Serving Size 1 1/3 tbsp (7g) makes 8 fl. oz., Servings 18, Calories 25, Fat Calories 0, Total Fat 0g, Saturated Fat 0g, Sodium 35mg, Total Carbohydrate 5g, **Sugars 0g,** Protein 0g. MAXWELL HOUSE COFFEE COMPANY, Kraft Foods, Inc.

NATURE'S PLUS® THE ENERGY SUPPLEMENTS® CAPPUCCINO.
Caffeine-free, Sugar-free SPIRU-TEIN® High Protein Energy Meal. Can be served hot or cold. Just add cow's milk, soy, or rice milk. Soy Protein Powder with Spirulina, Oat Bran, Apple Pectin, Bee Pollen, Enzymes, Vitamins, and Minerals. Vegetarian. Yeast Free. Sweetened with Fructose. Net Wt. 1.13 oz. (32g), Serving Size 1 Packet, Calories (with 1 cup skim milk) 180, Fat Calories 0, Total Fat 0, Saturated Fat 0g, Cholesterol 0mg, Sodium 140mg, Potassium 150mg, Total Carbohydrate 11g, Dietary Fiber 1g, **Sugars 8g**, Other Carbohydrate 2g, Protein 14g, and 15–140% of 22 vitamins and minerals. NATURAL ORGANICS, INC.

TEECCINO® CAFFEINE-FREE HERBAL COFFEE.
Contains No Coffee Beans. The first herbal coffee blended from herbs, grains, fruits and nuts that are roasted, ground and brewed just like coffee. Teeccino contains 65mg of potassium to give your body a natural energy lift. Ingredients: roasted carob, barley, chicory root, almonds, figs, dates, cocoa, & natural mocha flavor. No propylene glycol is used. Other flavors include Java, Chocolate Mint, Almond Amaretto, Vanilla Nut, Hazelnut, Mocha, Available at health food stores. ORIGINAL FLAVOR: Net Wt. 8.5 oz. (240g), Serving Size 1 Tb., Calories 20, Fat 0, Cholesterol 0mg, Sodium 2mg, Potassium 65mg, Total Carbohydrate 4g, **Sugars 2g**, Protein 0g, Caffeine 0mg. TEECCINO CAFFÉ, INC.

Decaffeinated Teas

A great Iced Tea available in a two serving bottle. Check your local grocer, health food market, or convenience store:

LONG LIFE® ICED TEAS DECAF GREEN TEA.
Lemon/Honey Wellness Infusion: Organic certified blends, fresh brewed in spring water. Ginkgo. Echinacea. Ginseng. GMO Free. Low Calorie. Low Sugar. Certified Kosher. Sodium Free. No Artificial Flavors, Preservatives, or Colors. Sweetened with Evaporated Cane Juice and Organic Honey. Net Wt. 16 oz. (1 pt.) 473 ml, Serving Size 8 fl. oz. (237 ml), Servings 2, Calories 50, Fat Calories 0, Total Fat 0g, Sodium 0mg, Total Carbohydrate 13g, **Sugars 13g**, Dietary Fiber 0g, Protein 0g. LONG LIFE TEAS.

BIGALOW® SWEET DREAMS® HERB TEA.
 No Caffeine. *"A relaxing blend of chamomile and hibiscus flowers . . . In the hustle and hurry that have become so much a part of our lives, it's important to take a moment at the end of each day to unwind. Sweet Dreams,® with its mild and soothing flavor, will add a peaceful note to the close of your day."* Many other flavors to choose from. R.C. BIGELOW, INC.

MAGIC MOUNTAIN® HERB TEA SWEET ORANGE SPICE.™
All Natural. No Caffeine. 16 Tea Bags. Net Wt. 1 oz. (28.5g). Rich flavor. Great price. The "tea of teas." MAGIC MOUNTAIN Herb Tea Co., Division of Boston Tea Co.

STASH® TEAS.
Decaffeinated. Flavorful! Economical too. Because there's so much flavor, one bag in a pot can make 2–3 cups. Many flavors including Spice, Mango Passion-fruit, Peppermint, Triple Ginseng, Wild Raspberry, and Wintermint. STASH TEA COMPANY

Hot Chocolate

SWISS MISS® NO SUGAR ADDED HOT COCOA MIX.
No Aspartame. No Saccharin. Low Fat. No Cholesterol. Sweetened with Sweet Dairy Whey, Maltodextrin, and Sucralose (Splenda® Brand). "This product contains only the natural sugars that come from milk. SPLENDA® Brand Sweetener adds no dietary sugar to this product. Available at your local grocery store. Eight .55 oz envelopes (Net Wt. 4.4 oz.) 125g, Serving Size 1 envelope (16g), Servings 8, Calories 60, Fat Calories 10, Total Fat

1g, Saturated Fat 0g, Cholesterol 0mg, Sodium 190mg, Total Carbohydrate 10g, Dietary Fiber 1g, **Sugars 6g**, Protein 2g, Calcium 30%, Iron 2%. *"Note:* Swiss Miss® also makes a "Diet" Hot Cocoa Mix that does contain Aspartame. It has less sugar and fewer calories. HUNT-WESSON, INC.

DUTCH CHOCOLATE COUNTRY LIFE® SOY-LICIOUS.™
A High Protein, Energizing Soy Powdered Drink. Fortified with Added Genistein & Daidzein. Rich Source of Antioxidants & Adaptogenic Herbs. Supplies All Essential Vitamins & Minerals. No Artificial Sweeteners. "Highest Soy Isoflavone Concentration of Any Soy Drink Available!" 150 mg Isoflavone per serving. Contains NovaSoy™ The Power of Soy™. Sweetened with Fructose. Available at your local health foods market. Net Wt. 1.3 oz. (38g), Serving Size 1 packet, Calories 140, Fat Calories 9, Total Fat 1g, Saturated Fat 0g, Cholesterol 0mg, Sodium 200mg, Potassium 250mg, Total Carbohydrate 18g, **Sugars 15g**, Protein 15g, and 20–200% of 22 vitamins and minerals. COUNTRY LIFE.

CARIBBEAN COCOA VEG LIFE® PEACEFUL PLANET.™
High Protein Energy Shake. 100% Vegetarian. 300 mg Calcium. Twice the Protein of Milk. 48 mg Soy Isoflavones. Sweetened with Fructose, Maltodextrin, and Malted Barley. Available at health food markets. Net Wt. 1.2 oz. (34g), Serving Size 1 packet, Calories 120, Fat Calories 10, Total Fat 1g, Saturated Fat 0g, Cholesterol 0mg, Sodium 170mg, Potassium 115mg, Total Carbohydrate 14g, Dietary Fiber 2g, **Sugars 9g**, Protein 16g, and 25 to 285% of 23 vitamins and minerals. VEG LIFE, INC.

These Chocolate Milks can be served Hot or Cold:

WHITE WAVE SILK™ CHOCOLATE SOY MILK.
Calcium enriched. Low 1% Fat & Vitamin Enriched. Certified GMO-free (Genetically Modified Organism) Soy. Sweetened with Naturally Milled Organic Cane. 1 quart (946 ml), Serving Size 1 cup (240 ml), Servings per container 4, Calories 130, Calories from Fat 20, Total Fat 2.5g, Saturated Fat 0g, Cholesterol 0mg, Sodium 75mg, Total Carbohydrate 23g, **Sugars 19g**, Protein 5g, Vitamin A 10%, Calcium 30%, Iron 2%, Riboflavin 30%, Vitamin D 30%, Vitamin B$_{12}$ 50%. Distributed by WHITE WAVE, INC.

VITASOY® LIGHT COCOA NATURAL SOY DRINK.
18mg Isoflavones per Serving. Made with Whole Organic Soybeans. 1% Fat. Reduced Calories. Sweetened with Cane Juice and Malt. Net Wt. 32 fl. oz. (1 qt.) 946ml, Serving Size 8 fl. oz. (240ml), Servings 4, Calories 80, Fat Calories 20, Total Fat 2g, Saturated Fat 1g, Polyunsaturated Fat 1g, Monounsaturated Fat 0.5g, Cholesterol 0mg, Sodium 130mg, Total Carbohydrate 13g, Dietary Fiber 1g, **Sugars 9g**, Other Carbohydrates 3g, Protein 4g, Calcium 6%, Iron 4%. VITASOY USA, INC.

VITASOY® LIGHT CAROB SUPREME NATURAL SOY DRINK. *31mg Isoflavones per Serving! Made with Whole Organic Soybeans. Cholesterol-free. Lactose-free. Dairy-free. No Artificial Preservatives, Sweeteners, Colors, or Flavors.* Sweetened with Cane Juice and Malt. Available at health food markets. Net Wt. 32 fl. oz. (1 qt.) 946ml, Serving Size 8 fl. oz. (240ml), Servings 4, Calories 150, Fat Calories 40, Total Fat 4.5g, Saturated Fat 1g, Polyunsaturated Fat 2.5g, Monounsaturated Fat 1g, Cholesterol 0mg, Sodium 160mg, Total Carbohydrate 22g, Dietary Fiber 1g, **Sugars 9g**, Other Carbohydrates 11g, Protein 7g, Calcium 6%, Iron 4%. VITASOY USA, INC.

BLUE DIAMOND® GROWER'S CO-OP™ ALMOND BREEZE.™ *Chocolate Non-Dairy Beverage made from real almonds. No Lactose. Only 1% Fat. Contains Calcium, Vitamins A, D, & E. Cholesterol Free.* Sweetened with Evaporated Cane Juice. Available at health food markets. 32 fl. oz. (1 qt.) 946 ml, Serving Size 8 fl. oz. (240 ml), Servings 4, Calories 120, Fat Calories 25, Total Fat 3g, Saturated Fat 0g, Cholesterol 0mg, Sodium 160mg, Potassium 180mg, Total Carbohydrate 21g, Dietary Fiber 1g, **Sugars 20g**, Protein 1g, Vitamin A 10%, Vitamin D 25%, Vitamin E 50%, Iron 4%, Calcium 20%. BLUE DIAMOND GROWERS.

A Healthier Chocolate Alternative:
(Carob is high in Isoflavones)

CHATFIELD'S CAROB & COMPLIMENTS CAROB POWDER. *A chocolate alternative for smoothies, hot drinks, or baking. No added sugar. Fat Free. Cholesterol Free. No caffeine. No chocolate or Cocoa.* No added sweeteners. Available at health food markets. Net Wt. 16 oz. (1 lb.), 454g, Serving size 1/4 cup, Servings per container 15, Calories 60, Fat Calories 0, Total Fat 0g, Saturated Fat 0g, Cholesterol 0mg, Sodium 10mg, Total Carbohydrate 27g, Fiber 3g, **Sugars 16g**, Protein 1g, Calcium 10%, Iron 4%. Distributed by: AMERICAN NATURAL SNACKS.

Flavored Syrups

Make your own flavored coffees!:

ATKINS™ SYRUPS. Sugar-free. All Natural Flavors. 0 Grams of Carbs per Serving. Available at health food markets. Syrup flavors include: Vanilla, Hazelnut, Chocolate, Strawberry, Cherry, Raspberry, and Maple. Sweetened with Sucralose. Net Wt. 12 fl. oz. (355 ml), Serving Size 1/4 Cup (2 fl. oz.) 60 ml, Servings 6, Calories 0, Fat Calories 0, Total Fat 0, Sodium 35mg (Chocolate 5mg), Total Carbohydrate 0g, **Sugars 0g**, Protein 0g. ATKINS NUTRITIONALS, INC.

Chapter 11
Protein Powder

P rotein powders are also available in bulk at most health food stores for a very economical price. Options include regular, soy-based, non-dairy, and vegetarian (no eggs or animal products).

Protein Powder

SCIENCE LABS NUTRITION™ SOY PROTEIN *POWDERED DRINK MIX. Dietary Supplement–Natural Vanilla Flavor with real Cranberry. 15 grams of Protein per serving. No added salt, yeast, wheat, preservatives, artificial flavors or colors.* Sweetened with Fructose, Lactose, Dextrose. Net Wt. 462g (16.30 oz.), Serving Size 1/3 cup (33g), Servings per container 14, Calories 120, Calories from Fat 10, Total Fat 1g, Total Carbohydrate 13g, **Sugars 8g**, Protein 15g, Calcium 56%, Iron 14%, Phosphorus 41%, Sodium (from soy protein isolate) 150mg (6%), Potassium 230mg (7%). Dried Cranberry Powder (from real cranberries) 1g. Manufactured by: WEIDER NUTRITION INTERNATIONAL.

WILD OATS™ ULTIMATE SOY-SPIRULINA PROTEIN POWDER.™
Supro® Soy Protein Powder Plus Earthrise® Spirulina. Vegetarian High Protein Energy Powder. *Contains no artificial colors, flavors, preservatives, corn, yeast, wheat, grain, egg, or milk products. Supports bone, cardiovascular, menopausal, and general health.* Sweetened with Fructose and Maltodextrin. Natural VANILLA flavor. Net Wt. 16 oz. (454g), Serving size one heaping scoop (30g), Servings per container about 15, Calories 110, Calories from Fat 7, Total Fat 1g, Saturated Fat 0g, Cholesterol 0mg, Sodium 143mg, Potassium 214mg, Total Carbohydrate 11g, Dietary Fiber 1g, **Sugars 9g**, Protein 15g. Plus 23 vitamins and minerals. WILD OATS MARKETS, INC.

BODY FORTRESS® PRECISION ENGINEERED WHEY PROTEIN™
Pure Whey Protein Powder. Easy to Assimilate. Glutamine Enriched. 98% Lactose Free. Low Calorie. No Aspartame. Yeast Free. No Preservatives, Soy, or Artificial Color. Contains the Amino Acids:

Isoleucine, Leucine, Valine. No Sucrose or Fructose added to this product. CHOCOLATE: Net Wt. 12 oz. (340g), Serving Size 1 scoop (23g), Servings 14, Calories 80, Fat Calories 10, Total Fat 1g, Saturated Fat 0.5g, Cholesterol 20mg, Sodium 200mg, Potassium 140mg, Total Carbohydrate 2g, Dietary Fiber 1g, **Sugars 1g**, Protein 17g, Calcium 15%, Thiamin 35%, Vitamin B_6 35%, Pantothenic Acid 35%, Riboflavin 35%, Vitamin B_{12} 35%, Phosphorus 10%. U.S. NUTRITION.

GENISOY® SOY PROTEIN POWDER

Natural. *The Magic of Soy® Fat-free, Soy Protein 24g per Serving. Isoflavones. Antioxidants. "Not a significant source of calories from fat, saturated fat, cholesterol, dietary fiber, and sugars."* Unsweetened. Net Wt. 17.8 oz. (504g), Serving Size 29g (1 scoop), Servings 17, Calories 100, Fat Calories (not listed), Total Fat 0g, Sodium 290mg, Potassium 90mg, Total Carbohydrate 0g, **Sugars 0g**, Protein 24g, and 25 – 170% of 19 Vitamins and Minerals. GENISOY PRODUCTS CO.

NATURE'S PLUS® *SPIRU-TEIN® SILVER.*

The Energy Supplements® *Rejuvenating Energy Formula for Mature Adults Healthy Heart Food™ Non-GMO Natural Soy™ Soy Protein Powder with Spirulina. Neuro-Nutrients, Energizing Herbs, Calcium, Enzymes, Vitamins, & Minerals. Mixes Instantly.* Sweetened with Fructose. *VANILLA:* Net Wt. 1.2 lbs. (544g), Serving Size 1 scoop (34g), Servings 16, Calories (with 1 cup skim milk) 179, Fat Calories 0, Total Fat 0, Saturated Fat 0g, Cholesterol 0mg, Sodium 150mg, Potassium 100mg, Total Carbohydrate 18g, Dietary Fiber 1g, **Sugars 12g**, Other Carbohydrate 5g, Protein 10g, and 15-250% of 22 Vitamins and Minerals. NATURAL ORGANICS, INC.

ATKINS® SHAKE MIX.

Sweetened with Sucralose. Flavors include: Chocolate, Strawberry, Vanilla, Cappucino. Net Wt. 16 oz. (454g), Serving Size 2 Scoops (43g), Servings 11, Calories 175, Fat Calories 76, Total Fat 8g, Saturated Fat 1g, Cholesterol 4mg, Sodium 160mg, Potassium 500mg, Total Carbohydrate 2g, Dietary Fiber 0g, **Sugars 1g**, Protein 23g. 40–100% of 15 Vitamins and Minerals. THE ATKINS CENTER.

The following products are available in both single serving packets and full-size canisters at your local natural foods market:

NATURE'S PLUS® SPIRU-TEIN® HIGH PROTEIN ENERGY MEAL.

The Energy Supplements® *Soy Protein Powder with Spirulina, Oat Bran, Apple Pectin, Bee Pollen, Enzymes, Vitamins, and Minerals. Vegetarian. Yeast Free.* CAPPUCCINO (Caffeine Free): Net Wt. 1.13 oz. (32g), Serving Size 1 Packet, Calories (with 1 cup skim milk) 180, Fat Calories 0, Total Fat 0, Saturated Fat 0g, Cholesterol 0mg, Sodium 140mg, Potassium 150mg, Total Carbohydrate 11g, Dietary

Fiber 1g, **Sugars 8g,** Other Carbohydrate 2g, Protein 14g, and 15–140% of 22 Vitamins and Minerals. Sweetened with Fructose. NATURAL ORGANICS, INC.

NATURE'S PLUS® VEGETARIAN FRUITEIN.®

The Energy Supplements.® *High Protein Low Calorie Energy Shake. All Natural Blend of Soy Protein, Vitamins, Minerals, Enzymes, and Whole Foods. Vegetarian. Yeast Free. Healthy Heart Food™ Non-GMO Natural Soy™* Sweetened with Fructose. BANANA ORANGE CREME: Net Wt. 1.2 oz. (34g), Serving Size 1 Packet, Calories 99, Fat Calories 0, Total Fat 0, Saturated Fat 0g, Cholesterol 0mg, Sodium 120mg, Potassium 110mg, Total Carbohydrate 15g, Dietary Fiber 1g, **Sugars 13g**, Other Carbohydrate 1g, Protein 10g, and 15-250% of 22 vitamins and minerals. NATURAL ORGANICS LABORATORIES, INC.

SOLARAY® SOYTEIN™ PROTEIN ENERGY MEAL.

Non-GMO. Good Source of Protein, Vitamins, and Minerals. Contains Fructose and Maltodextrin. STRAWBERRY: Net Wt. 31g, Serving Size 1 packet, Calories 100, Fat Calories 5, Total Fat 0.5g, Saturated Fat 0g, Cholesterol 0mg, Sodium 290mg, Potassium 250mg, Total Carbohydrate 11g, **Sugars 7g**, Protein 14g, and 15–250% of 22 vitamins and minerals. NUTRACEUTICAL CORP. for SOLARAY, INC.

COUNTRY LIFE® SOY-LICIOUS™

A High Protein, Energizing Soy Powdered Drink. Fortified with Added Genistein & Daidzein. Rich Source of Antioxidants & Adaptogenic Herbs. Supplies All Essential Vitamins & Minerals. No Artificial Sweeteners. "Highest Soy Isoflavone Concentration of Any Soy Drink Available!" 150 mg Isoflavone per serving. Contains NovaSoy™ The Power of Soy™ Sweetened with Fructose. DUTCH CHOCOLATE. Net Wt. 1.3 oz. (38g), Serving Size 1 packet, Calories 140, Fat Calories 9, Total Fat 1g, Saturated Fat 0g, Cholesterol 0mg, Sodium 200mg, Potassium 250mg, Total Carbohydrate 18g, **Sugars 15g**, Protein 15g, and 20-200% of 22 vitamins and minerals. COUNTRY LIFE.

VEG LIFE® PEACEFUL PLANET™ HIGH PROTEIN ENERGY SHAKE. *100% Vegetarian. 300 mg Calcium. Twice the Protein of Milk. 48 mg Soy Isoflavones.* Sweetened with Fructose, Maltodextrin, and Malted Barley. CARIBBEAN COCOA: Net Wt. 1.2 oz. (34g), Serving Size 1 packet, Calories 120, Fat Calories 10, Total Fat 1g, Saturated Fat 0g, Cholesterol 0mg, Sodium 170mg, Potassium 115mg, Total Carbohydrate 14g, Dietary Fiber 2g, **Sugars 9g**, Protein 16g, and 25-285% of 23 vitamins and minerals. VEG LIFE, INC.

Chapter 12
Frozen Delights

Frozen Fruit Juice Bars

DOLE® FRUIT JUICE QUIESCENTLY FROZEN JUICE BARS No Sugar Added. Flavors include: Strawberry, Grape, Raspberry. *Real fruit juice. Only 25 calories. Fat Free.* Sweetened with real Fruit, Fruit Juice Concentrate, Maltodextrin, Sorbitol and Aspartame (NutraSweet brand). 14 Bars (1.75 fl. oz.), Serving size 1 bar, Grape: Calories 25, Total Fat 0g, Sodium 5mg, Total Carbohydrate 6g, **Sugars 3g,** Sorbitol 2g, Vitamin C 25%. Distributed by: NESTLE' USA Food Group, Inc., Ice Cream Division, USA under license from Dole Packaged Foods Co.

TROPICANA® FRUIT JUICE BARS.
No Sugar Added. *Fat-free. 25 Calories per bar.* Sweetened with juice concentrate, Maltitol, Sorbitol, Aspartame, fruit puree. Variety Pack: Orange, Raspberry, Strawberry. Net Wt. 21 fl. oz. (621 ml), 12 Bars 1.75 fl. oz. (51.75 ml), Serving Size 1 Bar, Orange: Calories 25, Calories from Fat 0mg, Cholesterol 0mg, Sodium 0mg, Total Carbohydrate 5g, **Sugars 2g,** Sugar Alcohol 3g, Protein 0g, Vitamin A 8%, Vitamin C 10%. Mfd. under Authority of INTEGRATED BRANDS, INC., Under license from Tropicana Products, Inc.

Ice Cream Sandwiches

Our all-time favorite ice cream treat:

RICE DREAM® ICE CREAM PIE.
Rice Dream Ice Cream sandwiched between two oatmeal cookies with a chocolate coating. Non-Dairy. No Cholesterol. Sweetened with Brown Rice Syrup. Flavors: Mint, Vanilla, and Mocha. Net Wt. 3.7 fl. oz. (109 ml), Serving Size 88g, Servings 1 Pie, Calories 290, Calories from Fat 130, Total Fat 15g, Saturated Fat 7g, Cholesterol 0mg, Sodium 70mg, Total Carbohydrate 37g, Dietary Fiber 2g,

Sugars 13g, Protein 3g, Vitamin A 2%, Vitamin C 2%, Vitamin E 10%, Calcium 2%, Iron 6%. Distributed by: IMAGINE FOODS, INC.

GENUINE ESKIMO PIE® ICE CREAM SANDWICHES.
Reduced Fat Vanilla Ice Cream with Cookie Wafers–No sugar added. 60% Less Fat and 35% Less Calories than the leading ice cream sandwiches. Sweetened with Sorbitol, Maltodextrin, Polydextrose, and Aspartame (NutraSweet brand). Available in most grocery stores. 6 sandwiches 3.8 fl. oz. ea. (112 ml ea.) 22.8 fl. oz. (672 ml), Serving size 1 sandwich (65g), Calories 160, Calories from Fat 40, Total Fat 4g, Saturated Fat 2g, Cholesterol 10mg, Sodium 135mg, Total Carbohydrate 27g, Dietary Fiber 1g, **Sugars 4g**, Sugar Alcohols 8g, Protein 4g, Vitamin A 4%, Vitamin C 2%, Calcium 10%, Iron 4%. Manufactured under license from ESKIMO PIE Corporation.

WELLS® BLUE BUNNY™ ICE CREAM SANDWICHES.
Sweet Freedom™ No Sugar Added Ice Cream Sandwiches. Sweetened with Lactose (naturally occurring in dairy products), Polydextrose, Maltodextrin, Sorbitol, and Aspartame. Vanilla-flavored Reduced Fat Ice Cream between two Chocolate-flavored Wafers. 6 Sandwiches 3.5 fl. oz. (104 ml) each, Serving size 1 sandwich (66g), Calories 150, Calories from Fat 45, Total Fat 5g, Saturated Fat 2g, Cholesterol 10mg, Sodium 150mg, Potassium 105mg, Total Carbohydrate 25g, Dietary Fiber 1g, **Sugars 3g**, Sorbitol 6g, Protein 3g, Vitamin A 4%, Calcium 8%, Iron 2%. BLUE BUNNY, Manufactured by Wells' Dairy, Inc.

Sticks & Bars

How about a chocolate dipped nut sundae bar? It's hard to believe this one's all natural and good for you:

THE RICE DREAM® NUTTY BAR.
Non-Dairy. No Cholesterol. Vanilla Rice Dream Ice Cream Dipped in Chocolate and Covered in Peanuts. Unsweetened chocolate. Available at health food stores. Net Wt. 3.4 fl. oz. (100ml), Serving Size 1 Bar (86g), Calories 260, Fat Calories 160, Total Fat 18g, Saturated Fat 7g, Cholesterol 0mg, Sodium 55mg, Total Carbohydrate 23g, Dietary Fiber 2g, **Sugars 14g**, Protein 4g, Vitamin C 2%, Calcium 2%, Iron 4%. IMAGINE FOODS, INC.

THE RICE DREAM® BAR.
Chocolate Rice Dream Ice Cream Dipped in Chocolate, Non-Dairy. No Cholesterol. Unsweetened chocolate. Naturally sweetened with Barley and Corn Malt. Available at health food stores. Net Wt. 3.2 fl. oz. (95 ml), Serving Size 1 Bar (82g), Calories 200, Fat Calories 110, Total Fat 12g, Saturated Fat

10g, Cholesterol 0mg, Sodium 65mg, Total Carbohydrate 25g, Dietary Fiber 1g, **Sugars 16g,** Protein 2g, Vitamin C 2%, Calcium 2%, Iron 2%. IMAGINE FOODS, INC.

CHOCOLATE COVERED ICE CREAM BARS, WELLS® BLUE BUNNY.™ Sweet Freedom.™ *No Sugar-added Ice Cream Lites Vanilla flavored Lite Ice Cream with Dark Chocolate flavored Coating. 50% Less Fat than other leading bars. 45% Fewer Calories.* Sweetened with Lactose (naturally occurring in dairy products), Polydextrose, Maltodextrin, Sorbitol, Mannitol, Lactitol, and Aspartame. 12 Bars 2 fl. oz. (59.1 ml) each, Serving size 1 bar (40g), Calories 90, Calories from fat 50, Total Fat 6g, Saturated Fat 5g, Cholesterol 5mg, Sodium 55mg, Potassium 70mg, Total Carbohydrate 11g, **Sugars 2g,** Sugar Alcohol 4g, Protein 2g, Vitamin A 2%, Calcium 6%. BLUE BUNNY, Manufactured by Wells' Dairy, Inc.

CHOCOLATE COVERED CRISP RICE BARS, WELLS® BLUE BUNNY™ Sweet Freedom™ *No Sugar-added Krunch Lites. Vanilla flavored Lite Ice Cream with Chocolate flavored Coating and Crisp Rice.* Sweetened with Lactose (naturally occurring in dairy products), Polydextrose, Maltodextrin, Sorbitol, Mannitol, Lactitol, and Aspartame. 12 Bars 2 fl. oz. (59.1 ml) each, Serving size 1 bar (41g), Calories 90, Calories from Fat 50, Total Fat 6g, Saturated Fat 5g, Cholesterol 5mg, Sodium 60mg, Potassium 70mg, Total Carbohydrate 11g, **Sugars 2g,** Sugar Alcohol 4g, Protein 2g, Vitamin A 2%, Calcium 6%. BLUE BUNNY, Wells' Dairy, Inc.

GENUINE ESKIMO PIE® CRISPED RICE ICE CREAM BARS. *Reduced-fat Vanilla Ice Cream Bars Dipped in a Milk Chocolate Flavored Coating with Crisped Rice–No Sugar Added. 40% Less Fat and Calories than the leading ice cream bars.* Sweetened with Sorbitol, Maltodextrin, Mannitol, Polydextrose, and Aspartame (NutraSweet Brand). Available in most grocery stores. Net Wt. 15 fl. oz. (444 ml), 6 Bars 2.5 fl. oz. ea. (74 ml ea), Serving size 1 Bar, Calories 120, Calories from fat 70, Total Fat 8g, Saturated Fat 7g, Cholesterol 10mg, Sodium 40mg, Total Carbohydrate 13g, Dietary Fiber 0g, **Sugars 3g,** Sugar Alcohols 2g, Protein 3g, Vitamin A 4%, Calcium 8%. *This product contains no Sucrose but does contain Lactose, a naturally occurring sugar in dairy products.* Manufactured under license from ESKIMO PIE CORPORATION.

GENUINE ESKIMO PIE® ICE CREAM BARS.
Reduced Fat Vanilla Ice Cream Bars Dipped in a Milk Chocolate Flavored Coating–*No Sugar Added. 40% Less Fat and Calories than the leading ice cream bars.* Sweetened with Sorbitol, Maltodextrin, Mannitol, Polydextrose, and Aspartame (NutraSweet Brand). *This product contains no Sucrose but does contain Lactose, a naturally occurring sugar in dairy products.* Available in most grocery stores. Net Wt. 15 fl. oz. (444 ml), 6 Bars 2.5 fl. oz. ea. (74 ml ea.), Serving size 1 Bar, Calories 120, Calories from Fat 70, Total

Fat 8g, Saturated Fat 6g, Cholesterol 10mg, Sodium 40mg, Total Carbohydrate 13g, Dietary Fiber 0g, **Sugars 4g,** Sugar Alcohols 2g, Protein 3g, Vitamin A 4%, Calcium 8%. Manufactured under license from ESKIMO PIE Corporation

Sherbet on a stick!

FAT-FREE CREME BARS WELLS® BLUE BUNNY™

No sugar added. Health Smart® Sweetened with Sorbitol. Flavors: frozen Raspberry, frozen Orange, Rainbow, Fat-free Fudge Bars, Vanilla Nutty Sundae Cones, and Sweet Freedom® Fruit Juice Lites. Six Bars 2.5 fl. oz. (73.9ml), Serving Size 1 bar (66g), Amount Per Serving: Calories 70, Calories from Fat 0, Total Fat 0g, Saturated Gat 0g, Cholesterol 0mg, Sodium 35mg, Potassium 70mg, Total Carbohydrate 18g, **Sugars 2g,** Protein 2g, Vitamin A 10% D.V., Calcium 4% D.V. *Attn. Diabetics: The small amount of sugar in Health Smart® comes from lactose which is a naturally occurring sugar in the milk used to produce this product.* BLUE BUNNY.

SUPERBRAND® FUDGE POPS.

No Sugar Added. *Quiescently Frozen Confections.* Sweetened with Maltodextrin, Polydextrose, Aspartame. Available at grocery stores. Serving size 1 bar (50g), Servings per container 12, Calories 50, Calories from Fat 10, Total Fat 1g, Saturated Fat 0.5g, Cholesterol 0mg, Sodium 35mg, Total Carbohydrate 11g, **Sugars 3g,** Protein 2g, Calcium 8% DV. WINN-DIXIE STORES, INC.

I Scream for Ice Cream

Our family favorite:

BREYER'S® NO SUGAR ADDED VANILLA ICE CREAM.

Contains real vanilla bean specks. *Light Ice Cream–Half the Fat and 45% Less Calories than regular ice cream.* Sweetened with naturally occurring Lactose in dairy, Maltodextrin, Polydextrose, and Aspartame. Half Gallon (1.89l), Serving size 1/2 cup (69g), Servings per container 16, Calories 90, Calories from Fat 40, Total Fat 4.5g, Saturated Fat 2.5g, Cholesterol 25mg, Sodium 50mg, Total Carbohydrate 11g, **Sugar 6g,** Sugar Alcohol 1g, Protein 3g, Vitamin A 6%, Calcium 10%. GOOD HUMOR/BREYER'S ICE CREAM.

My favorite flavor!

TIN ROOF SUNDAE, WELLS® BLUE BUNNY™

No Sugar Added, reduced-fat Ice Cream. *"Vanilla Flavored Reduced-Fat Ice Cream Swirled with a Chocolate Fudge Ribbon and Chocolate Covered Peanuts–30% Less Fat Than Our Premium Ice Cream."* Sweetened with Sorbitol, Aspartame, Polydextrose, Mannitol, naturally occuring Lactose and Maltodextrin. Half Gallon (1.89l), Serving Size 1/2 Cup (73g), Servings 16, Calories 140, Calories from Fat 60, Total Fat 6g, Saturated Fat 3.5g, Cholesterol 15mg, Sodium 80mg, Potassium 150mg, Total Carbohydrate 20g, **Sugars 4g,** Sugar Alcohol 7g, Protein 4g, Vitamin A 4%, Calcium 8%. WELLS' BLUE BUNNY.

EDY'S® CHIPS 'N SWIRLS™ NO SUGAR ADDED LIGHT ICE CREAM. *"Vanilla light ice cream with swirls of caramel and chocolatey chips."* Natural and artificial flavors added. Sweetened with Sorbitol, Maltodextrin, Poydextrose, naturally occurring Lactose (a dairy sugar), and Aspartame. Other flavors available. Half Gallon (1.89l), Serving size 1/2 cup (62g), Servings per container 16, Calories 100, Calories from Fat 25, Total Fat 3g, Saturated Fat 1.5g, Cholesterol 10mg, Sodium 60mg, Total Carbohydrate 16g, **Sugars 3g**, Sugar Alcohols 7g, Protein 3g, Vitamin A 8% DV, Calcium 6% DV. Manufactured by: EDY'S GRAND ICE CREAM.®

EDY'S® BLUEBERRY COBBLER.™
No Sugar Added Fat Free Light Ice Cream. *"Vanilla Fat Free ice cream with Blueberry swirls and Cobbler Pieces."* Natural and artificial flavors added. Sweetened with Sorbitol, Maltodextrin, Poydextrose, naturally occurring Lactose (a dairy sugar), and Aspartame. Other flavors available. Half Gallon (1.89l), Serving size 1/2 cup (62g), Servings per container 16, Calories 100, Calories from fat 0, Total Fat 0g, Saturated Fat 0g, Cholesterol 5mg, Sodium 60mg, Total Carbohydrate 22g, **Sugars 4g**, Sugar Alcohols 5g, Protein 3g, Vitamin A 6% DV, Calcium 6%. Manufactured by: EDY'S GRAND ICE CREAM

Be sure to differentiate between "Light" and "No Sugar Added." Count sugar grams and servings. This flavor has a little more sugar than the "No Added Sugar" version so go easy. As a once-in-awhile treat, it can't be beat.

EDY'S® FRENCH SILK™ GRAND LIGHT® ICE CREAM.
Chocolate Mocha Mousse Light Ice Cream with Chocolate Chips Swirled with Vanilla Mousse Light Ice Cream. Sweetened with Sugar, Corn Syrup, Dextrose. Half Gallon (1.89ltr.), Serving Size 1/2 cup, Servings 16, Calories 120, Calories from Fat 35, Total Fat 4g, Saturated Fat 3.0g, Cholesterol 15mg, Sodium 50mg, Total Carbohydrate 19g, **Sugars 14g**, Protein 3g, Vitamin A 4%, Calcium 6%. EDY'S GRAND ICE CREAM.

This flavor is sometimes referred to as Neopolitan:

BREYER'S® NO SUGAR ADDED VANILLA - CHOCOLATE - STRAWBERRY ICE CREAM. *Light Ice Cream–Half the Fat and 40% Less Calories than regular ice cream.* Sweetened with naturally occurring

Lactose in dairy, Maltodextrin, Polydextrose, and Aspartame. Half Gallon (1.89 ltr.), Serving size 1/2 cup (69g), Servings per container 16, Calories 90, Calories from Fat 40, Total Fat 4.5g, Saturated Fat 2.5g, Cholesterol 25mg, Sodium 45mg, Total Carbohydrate 11g, **Sugar 6g,** Sugar Alcohol 1g, Protein 3g, Vitamin A 6%, Calcium 10%. GOOD HUMOR/ BREYER'S ICE CREAM.

All Natural:

RICE DREAM® NON-DAIRY DESSERT
MINT CAROB CHIP: One Pint 473 ml. Parevine, Serving Size 1/2 Cup (92g), Servings 4, Calories 170, Calories from Fat 70, Total Fat 8g, Saturated Fat 2g, Cholesterol 0mg, Sodium 95mg, Total Carbohydrate 26g, Dietary Fiber 1g, **Sugars 18g,** Protein 1g, Vitamin A 2%, Calcium 2%, Vitamin C 2%, Iron 4%. Sweetened with Brown Rice and Whole Grain Malted Barley. IMAGINE FOODS, INC.

Chapter 13
Jams and Jellies

Jams and Jellies

TREE OF LIFE® 100% FRUIT.
Contains whole fruit and fruit sweetened with fruit juice concentrate only.
STRAWBERRY FANCY FRUIT SPREAD. Other flavors include: Peach, Raspberry, Grape, Cherry, Blueberry, Apricot. Net Wt. 10 oz. (284g), Serving Size 1 tbsp. (18g), Servings 16, Calories 35, Fat Calories 0g, Sodium 0mg, Total Carbohydrate 9g, **Sugars 9g**, Protein 0g. TREE OF LIFE, INC.

HARVEST MOON™ ORGANIC FRUIT SPREAD.
Ingredients: Organic White Grape Juice Concentrate, Organic Raspberries, Lemon Juice Concentrate, Natural Fruit Pectin. RASPBERRY: Net Wt 10 oz. (283g), Serving size 1 tbsp. (18g), Servings 16, Calories 35, Fat Calories 0, Total Fat 0g, Sodium 0mg, Total Carbohydrate 9g, **Sugars 9g**, Protein 0g. TREE OF LIFE, INC.

SEEDLESS BLACKBERRY JAM POLANER® All Fruit®
Spreadable Fruit. Many flavors. Sweetened only with fruit and fruit juice concentrate. All natural. Fruit sweetened. Net Wt. 10oz. (285g), Serving size 1 tbsp. (18g), Servings Per Container About 16, Calories 40, Calories from Fat 0, Total Fat 0g, Sodium 0mg, Total Carbohydrate 10g, **Sugars 9g**, Protein 0g. M. POLANER, INC./International Home Foods, Inc.

SMUCKER'S® LIGHT SUGAR-FREE SEEDLESS BLACKBERRY JAM. 80% Fewer Calories Than Regular Preserves. Fat-free. Cholesterol-free. Sweetened with Fruit, Polydextrose, Maltodextrin, and Aspartame. Net Wt 12.75 oz. (361g), Serving size 1 Tbsp. (17g), Servings 21, Calories 10. Not a significant source of calories from fat, saturated fat, cholesterol, dietary fiber, vitamin A, vitamin C, calcium, and iron. Total Fat 0g, Sodium 0mg, Total Carbohydrate 5g, **Sugars 0g**, Protein 0g. J. M. SMUCKER CO. *A Proud Sponsor of the American Diabetes Association*®

SMUCKER'S® LOW SUGAR CONCORD GRAPE.
Reduced-sugar jelly. *Half the sugar of regular jelly. Fat-free. Cholesterol-free.* Sweetened with Grape Juice and Sugar. Net Wt. 15.5 oz. (440g), Serving size 1 Tbsp. (17g), Servings 25, Calories 25. Not a significant source of calories from fat, saturated fat, cholesterol, dietary fiber, vitamin A, vitamin C, calcium, and iron. Total Fat 0g, Sodium 0mg, Total Carbohydrate 6g, **Sugars 5g**, Protein 0g. J. M. SMUCKER CO.

TAP'N APPLE® APPLE BUTTER SPREAD.
All Natural. No Preservatives. Naturally Fat-free. Cholesterol-free. Sodium-free. Nothing Artificial Added. No added sweeteners. Net Wt. 18 oz. (510g), Serving Size 1 Tsp. (16g), Servings about 31, Calories 20, Fat Calories 0, Total Fat 0g, Saturated Fat 0g, Cholesterol 0mg, Sodium 0mg, Total Carbohydrate 5g, Dietary Fiber 1g, **Sugars 4g**, Protein 0g. LIBERTY RICHTER.

SWEET NOTHINGS™ SUGAR FREE LITE PRESERVES.
60% Fewer Calories than Regular Preserves. No Aspartame. No Saccharin. Sweetened with Maltitol and Fruit. Net Wt. 9.5 oz. (269g), Serving Size 1 Tbsp. (17g), Servings 15, Calories 20, Total Fat 0, Sodium 5mg, Total Carbohydrate 6g, **Sugars 0g,** Maltitol 5g, Protein 0g. BORN FREE FOODS, INC.

Chapter 14
Pudding and Jello

Pudding & Jello

IMAGINE NATURAL® BUTTERSCOTCH PUDDING CUPS.
100% All Natural Snack. Low Fat & Non-Dairy. Lactose Free. "Healthy Kid's Snack–Delicious Creamy Taste–Needs No Refrigeration." Sweetened with Brown Rice Syrup. Available at your health food market. Other flavors: Chocolate. Net Wt. 15 oz. (425g), 4-3.75 oz Cups, Serving Size 1 cup (106g), Calories 140, Fat Calories 25, Total Fat 3g, Saturated Fat 0g, Cholesterol 0mg, Sodium 55mg, Total Carbohydrate 28g, **Sugars 16g**, Protein 1g, Vitamin E 4%, Iron 2%. IMAGINE FOODS, INC.

SUGAR FREE VANILLA PUDDING.
ROYAL® Pudding and Pie Filling. *33% Fewer calories than regular pudding (100 vs. 150.)* Artificially sweetened. Available at grocery stores. Other flavors include Chocolate and White Chocolate. Net Wt. 1.7 oz. (48g), Serving size 1/2 cup (12g), Servings per container 4, Calories 40 (with 2% milk, 100), Fat calories with milk 20, Total Fat 0g, Saturated Fat 0g, Cholesterol 0g, Sodium 410mg, Total Carbohydrate 10g, **Sugars 0g**, Protein 0g, Vitamin A 6% DV, Vitamin C 2% DV, Calcium 15% DV, Iron 2% DV. Distributed by: NABISCO.

ROYAL® PISTACHIO PUDDING AND PIE FILLING.
Sugar-free pudding. *Fat Free. Reduced Calorie. 33% Fewer calories than regular pudding.* Sweetened with Maltodextrin (from corn), Aspartame and Acesulfame Potassium. Available at grocery stores. Other flavors include Chocolate and White Chocolate. Net Wt. 1.7 oz. (48g), Serving size 1/2 cup (12g), Servings per container 4, Calories 100 (with 2% Milk), Fat calories 25, Total Fat 0.5g, Saturated Fat 0g, Cholesterol 0g, Sodium 410mg, Total Carbohydrate 9g, **Sugars 0g**, Protein 0g, Vitamin A 6%, Vitamin C 2%, Calcium 15%, Iron 0%. Distributed by: NABISCO Foods.

JELL-0® FAT-FREE, SUGAR-FREE, INSTANT REDUCED-CALORIE PUDDING & PIE FILLING. 1/3 fewer calories than regular pudding. Sweetened with Maltodextrin (from corn), Aspartame and Acesulfame Potassium. Available at grocery stores. VANILLA (many other flavors). Net Wt. 1 oz. (28g), Serving size 1/4 package (8g), Servings per container 4, Calories 70 (with Fat Free Milk), Fat calories 0, Total Fat 0g, Saturated Fat 0g, Cholesterol 0g, Sodium 330mg, Total Carbohydrate 6g, **Sugars 0g**, Protein 0g, Vitamin A 4%, Vitamin C 0%, Calcium 15%, Iron 0%. Distributed by: KRAFT FOODS, INC. *JELL-0® Brand also produces many other wonderful sugar-free Jello® desserts. A Proud Sponsor of the American Diabetes Association.*

Chapter 15
Yogurt

Another healthy choice for yogurt is, of course, to buy plain yogurt and sweeten it yourself with fresh fruit, real vanilla extract, or honey. But, for convenience sake premixed yogurts sealed in small containers are great. Still, you might want to add some unsweetened granola, nuts, or seeds to make them an even healthier snack. Do be aware that most low-sugar yogurts are presently being sweetened with aspartame.

Remember that yogurt contains lactose, a natural dairy sugar. The best sugar content will be around eight to twelve grams per serving. You will be surprised to find that some of your favorite varieties can contain as much as forty-nine grams of sugar per serving.

If you would like to try some all-natural yogurts or soy yogurt, visit your local health food market. Be aware however, that often these varieties do have a high sugar content, albeit natural sugars. As always, check your labels carefully and know that natural sugars do metabolize more slowly.

Nonfat Dairy Yogurt

GREAT VALUE™ LIGHT NONFAT YOGURT, LEMON CHIFFON. *Contains aspartame and natural flavors. Half the calories of sugar sweetened nonfat yogurt.* Sweetened with naturally occurring Lactose in dairy, Corn Syrup, and Aspartame. Many more flavors include: Banana Cream Pie and Vanilla. Net Wt. 6 oz. (170g), Grade A, Serving size one container, Calories 80 (regular sugar sweetened yogurt 160), Fat Calories 0, Total Fat 0g, Saturated Fat 0g, Cholesterol 0mg, Sodium 75mg, Potassium 280mg, Total Carbohydrate 13g, **Sugars 8g**, Protein 6g, Calcium 20%. Marketed by: WALMART® Stores, Inc.

SUPERBRAND® NONFAT YOGURT

Nonfat Yogurt with aspartame and natural flavors. Sweetened with naturally occurring Lactose in dairy, Fruit, Maltitol Syrup, Maltodextrin, and Aspartame. Flavors include: Cherry Amaretto Cheesecake, Black Cherry, Raspberry, Strawberry Banana, Strawberry-kiwi, Key Lime Pie, Strawberry, Apricot, Mango, and more. Net Wt. 8 oz. (227g), Grade-A Pasteurized, Serving size one container, Calories 90 (regular sugar-sweetened yogurt 210), Fat Calories 0, Total Fat 0g, Saturated Fat 0g, Cholesterol 0mg, Sodium 130mg, Potassium 360mg, Total Carbohydrate 14g, **Sugars 11g**, Protein 9g, Calcium 30%. WINN-DIXIE STORES.

Lowfat Organic Yogurt

STONYFIELD FARM® ORGANIC LOW-FAT YOGURT 99% Fat Free. 1% Milk Fat. Organic standards prohibit the use of pesticides, antibiotics, and hormones. Sweetened with Organic Maple Syrup. MAPLE VANILLA: Net Wt 6 oz (170g), Serving size 1 container, Calories 120, Fat Calories 15, Total Fat 1.5g, Saturated Fat 1g, Cholesterol 5mg, Sodium 95mg, Total Carbohydrate 19, **Sugars 19g**, Protein 6g, Vitamin C 2%, Calcium 30%, Iron 2%. STONYFIELD FARM YOGURT.

Soy Yogurt

WHOLESOY® CREAMY CULTURED SOY.

Non-Dairy, Lactose Free, and No Cholesterol. Isoflavones: 23mg. Sweetened with Organic Raw Cane Crystals and Fruit. *Other flavors include Raspberry, and Peach. Live active cultures. Natural flavors.* STRAWBERRY: Net Wt. 6 oz. (170g), Serving size 1 container, Calories 140, Fat Calories 20, Total Fat 2.5g, Saturated Fat 0g, Cholesterol 0mg, Sodium 20mg, Total Carbohydrate 27g, Dietary Fiber 1g, **Sugars 19g**, Protein 5g, Calcium 8%, Iron 6%. Distributed by: WHOLESOY® *10% of profits given to the planet.*

Chapter 16
Alcohol Alternatives

A lcohol can cause severely low blood sugar, even in individuals without diabetes or hypoglycemia, and it can become life-threatening. Never have a drink without having some food at the same time. Studies have shown that alcohol taken with food may actually be beneficial for some people; but most of these studies are with *healthy* people—not diabetics or hypoglycemics. Be cautious. Since alcohol reduces blood sugar, hypoglycemics and diabetics should NEVER have a drink.

In *Patient Care* magazine, Richard Birrer writes that alcohol is the usual reason for hypoglycemic complications in diabetic patients, aged eleven to thirty. The most common reason for hypoglycemic coma, in patients aged thirty to fifty, is alcohol taken either alone or in combination with insulin.

Spirits Anyone?

Before I understood the danger of alcohol consumption to my hypoglycemic condition, my husband and I decided to relive our honeymoon experience in Hawaii by making Mai Tais. Unfortunately, I accidentally bought 100 proof dark rum (red rum). After one drink I began to fade. We had prepared T-bone steaks for this anniversary celebration and the last thing I remember, before I passed out, was the sight of our cat, Aleister, dragging my steak across the living room carpet. I couldn't move. And my husband wasn't any help either because he was rolling on the floor with laughter.

When I awakened there was a litany inside my head. It was the "red rum" chant from the movie, *The Shining*, and it proceeded to keep me awake throughout the night. "Red rum" spelled backwards, of course, is *murder*. I was terrified as I relived the intense fear-based emotions of that film. This type of anxiety episode was not unusual for me.

If I had understood the hypoglycemic effect of alcohol I would have known that a well-balanced meal could have restored my glucose level, and thus, relieved me of the tortuous mental anguish that I was experiencing. Instead, I suffered from recurring panic attacks and anxiety episodes for years. Even a minimum amount of alcohol can induce symptoms in a hypoglycemic.

What to Drink

As substitutes for alcohol you can order plain water or soda water with a lemon wedge or twist of lime to simulate a mixed drink. Another favorite substitute is juice, such as unsweetened grapefruit juice, because it is lower in sugar than orange juice. Mix it with soda and a twist of lime to mimic a Fuzzy Navel type drink. Bartenders are usually very happy to serve nonalcoholic versions of common mixed drinks. Here's another bonus for remaining alcohol-free: assign yourself the position of designated driver and you'll get your non-alcoholic drinks for free.

My favorite option is a nonalcoholic "Bloody Mary"; sometimes called a "Virgin Mary." It is essentially spicy tomato juice and is extremely low glycemic. For very special occasions I indulge by having a nonalcoholic frozen "Virgin Lime Margarita" with no salt. The margarita sour mix does contain some sugar so I limit these to one. I used to love the sweet drinks like Piña Coladas, Daiquiris, and Port. But they are now off limits. If you want to order a clear soft drink or a cola, be sure that they are both "diet" (sugar-free) and caffeine free. Since most diet sodas contain aspartame, please read Chapter 1: Aspartame, for possible side effects.

Chapter 17
Soft Drinks

Soft drinks contain nearly a teaspoon of sugar for every ounce. So a thirty-two ounce drink will have around thirty teaspoons of sugar! The average person drinks nearly five-hundred cans of soda pop per year. The average teenager, about three and one half cans of soda a day. This is in addition to a diet loaded with refined sugar, white foods, and rancid fats. What can we do? We can make better choices more readily available.

Acceptable soft drinks are those with neither sugar nor caffeine. But even these should be limited as diet drinks may also contain harmful ingredients such as phosphoric acid, aspartame, and a good amount of sodium. Water is always the best choice. It should be your staple choice for hydration. To make it palatable try adding a wedge of lemon or lime. A squirt of lemonade or iced tea added to water is also refreshing. A citrus wedge adds Vitamin C.

Avoid distilled water because it lacks the minerals needed for absorption into the body. Choose purified or spring water whenever possible, but generally, most tap water is safe for consumption unless it has a bad taste or smell. It is more important that you never miss an opportunity for hydration. Please read *Your Body's Many Cries For Water: You Are Not Sick, You Are Thirsty* by Fereydoon Batmanghelidj (Global Health Solutions).

My husband and I have made ordering water a habit when dining out. It was not our first choice, but it is difficult to find sugar-free and caffeine-free drinks at restaurants. Soda water or sparkling flavored waters may be other alternatives, but be careful. Check the label for excess sodium and sugar content. Flavored waters can often be high in added sugars.

Your health food store may have fruit juice-flavored sodas and teas. But these may also be high in natural sugar, some as much as 39 grams per serving! Remember, if you have symptoms of any kind, you should have no more than twelve grams of sugar per serving in naturally sweetened foods, and no more than three grams per serving of foods with real sugar (preferably none at all).

Milk is another option. With the best choice being low-fat cow's milk, rice, almond, or soy milk. Another option is juice. However, juice should generally be avoided because of its high concentration of sugar. It can be as high as thirty to forty grams per glass! If you must have juice, dilute it with water or choose tomato or unsweetened grapefruit juice. It is preferable to drink it first thing in the morning, before a well-balanced breakfast.

Let me be perfectly clear. Soft drinks are *not* good for you, although you my drink them occasionally without too much harm. My definition of occasionally is *less* than once a month. Remember, even a drink that is labeled *diet* may contain harmful ingredients (See Chapter 1). Consume them at your own risk.

Chapter 18
Other Healthy Options

S ome of the products and packaged meals listed are not whole grain. I have included them, however, as the best choices for your transitional diet. Sometimes whole grain items are simply unavailable. Your best bet for finding whole grain foods is your health foods market.

Canned Goods

YELLOW CLING SLICED PEACHES, NO SUGAR ADDED.
Libby's® Natural Lite™ *In real fruit juice from concentrate. No sugar added. 40% less calories than yellow cling peaches in heavy syrup.* Net Wt. 15oz. (425g), Serving Size 1/2 cup, Servings per container 3.5, Calories 60, Calories from Fat 0, Total Fat 0g, Saturated Fat 0g, Cholesterol 0mg, Sodium 10mg, Potassium 105mg, Total Carbohydrate 13g, Dietary Fiber 1g, **Sugars 12g**, Protein 1g, Vitamin A 6% DV, Vitamin C 2% DV. Distributed by: TRI VALLEY GROWERS.

Chips

GARDEN OF EATIN'® BLUE CHIPS ALL NATURAL TORTILLA CHIPS. No Salt Added. Made with Organic Blue Corn. Also available SESAME BLUES® All Natural Tortilla Chips with Sesame Seeds. Net Wt. 9 oz. (255g), Serving Size 1 oz. (28g/about 16 chips), Servings Per Container 9, Calories 150, Fat Calories 60, Total Fat 7g, Saturated Fat .5g, Cholesterol 0mg, Sodium 10mg, Total Carbohydrate 18g, Dietary Fiber 1g, **Sugars 0g**, Protein 2g, Calcium 4%, Iron 4%. GARDEN OF EATIN'/Corporate HQ–THE HAIN FOOD GROUP, INC.

Dessert Topping

KRAFT® COOL WHIP LITE® WHIPPED TOPPING.
50% Less fat than average whipped topping. Sweetened with Corn Syrup and High Fructose Corn Syrup. Net Wt. 8 oz. (226g), Serving size 2 Tbsp. (9g),

Calories 20, Fat Calories 10, Total Fat 1g, Saturated 1g, Sodium 0mg, Total Carbohydrate 3g, **Sugars 1g**, Protein 0g. KRAFT FOODS, INC.

Better Than Butter

We love this stuff! Tastes great and melts like real butter:

SMART BALANCE® NON-HYDROGENATED BUTTERY SPREAD.
"Patented Blend To Help Improve Cholesterol Ratio. No trans-fatty-acids –naturally!" 67% natural vegetable oils. Based on Brandeis University cholesterol research. Net Wt. 16 oz. (1 lb.) 454 g, Serving Size 1 Tbsp. (14g), Servings per container 32, Calories 80, Calories from Fat 80, Total Fat 9g, Saturated Fat 2.5g, Polyunsaturated Fat 2.5g, Monounsaturated Fat 3.5g, Cholesterol 0mg, Sodium 90mg, Total Carbohydrate 0g, Protein 0g, Vitamin A 10%, Vitamin E 10%. Owned and distributed by: GFA BRANDS, INC.

Milk

ORGANIC VALLEY™ LOW FAT COW'S MILK.
Produced without hormones, antibiotics, or pesticides. Grade A, Ultra-Pasteurized, Homogenized. Half Gallon (1.89 ltr.), Serving Size 1 cup (240 ml), Calories 100, Calories from Fat 20, Total Fat 2.5g, Saturated Fat 1.5g, Cholesterol 10mg, Sodium 120mg, Total Carbohydrate 12g, **Sugars 12**, Protein 8g, Vitamin A 10%, Vitamin C 2%, Calcium 30%, Vitamin D 25%. Naturally occurring lactose. www.organicvalley.com CROPP COOPERATIVE, La Barge, Wisconsin 54639.

(See also Chapter 9—Drinks: Soy Milk, Rice Milk, Almond Milk, Chocolate Milk)

Miscellaneous

AM"'S® SPINACH FETA POCKET SANDWICH.
Organic Spinach & Feta Cheese, in an organic whole wheat pocket sandwich. Net Wt. 4.5 oz. (128g), Serving Size 1 sandwich, Calories 250, Fat Calories 80, Total Fat 9g, Saturated Fat 4.5g, Cholesterol 20mg, Sodium 590mg, Total Carbohydrate 34g, Dietary Fiber 3g, **Sugars 4g**, Protein 11g, Vitamin A 80%, Calcium 25%, Vitamin C 10%, Iron 20%. AMY'S KITCHEN, INC.

MORNING STAR FARMS® MEAT-FREE CORN DOGS.
"America's Original Veggie Dog™ Batter-Dipped on Stick." 67% Less Fat than meat corn dogs, No Cholesterol. Net Wt. 10 oz. (284g), Serving Size 1 Dog (71g), Servings 4, Calories 150, Calories from Fat 30, Total Fat 4g, Saturated Fat 0.5g,

Polyunsaturated Fat 2.5g, Monounsaturated Fat 1g, Cholesterol 0mg, Sodium 500mg, Potassium 60mg, Total Carbohydrate 22g, Dietary Fiber 3g, **Sugars 4g**, Protein 7g, Iron 6%. Contains Sugar, Dextrose, Corn Syrup Solids. WORTHINGTON FOODS, INC.

MORNING STAR FARMS® VEGETARIAN HOT DOGS

"America's Original Veggie Dog"™ Additional MORNINGSTAR FARMS® choices include: Better'n Burger,® Quarter Prime,™ or Grillers® Meat-Free Burger, Breakfast Links and Patties, Garden Veggie Patties® or Hard Rock Cafe® Burgers. Vegetarian HOT DOGS: Low Fat. No Cholesterol. Net Wt. 1 lb. (454g), Serving Size 1 Dog (57g), Servings 8, Calories 80, Calories from Fat 5, Total Fat 0.5g, Saturated Fat 0g, Cholesterol 0mg, Sodium 580mg, Potassium 60mg, Total Carbohydrate 6g, Dietary Fiber 1g, **Sugars 2g**, Protein 11g, Iron 4%. Contains Brown Sugar, Dextrose, Corn Syrup Solids. WORTHINGTON FOODS, INC.

LIGHTLIFE® TEMPEH ORGANIC WILD RICE.

A High Protein Soy Product. 19 Grams of Protein. High in Iron. No Cholesterol. Can be sautéed, grated, stewed, or baked for a variety of main courses from sandwiches to stir fry's. Other flavors available. Net Wt. 8 oz. (224g), Serving Size 4 oz (113g), Servings 2, Calories 190, Fat Calories 60, Total Fat 7g, Saturated Fat 1g, Cholesterol 0mg, Sodium 0mg, Total Carbohydrate 13g, Dietary Fiber 6g, **Sugars 3g,** Protein 19g, Calcium 10%, Vitamin C 2%, Iron 30%. Ingredients: Organically grown soybeans, water, organic wild rice, organic brown rice, tempeh culture. LIGHTLIFE FOODS, INC.

HALLS® MENTHO-LYPTUS® SUGAR FREE MENTHOL COUGH SUPPRESSANT. Contains Aspartame and Isomalt. Flavors: Citrus blend, Mountain Menthol, or Black Cherry. 25 Drops. Distriubuted by: WARNER-LAMBERT COMPANY.

ZAND® HERBAL LOZENGE .

Sweetened Only with Natural Rice Syrup, No Cane Sugar, No Fructose, No Artitfical Sweeteners. Flavors: Lemon, Cherry Echinacea Zinc lozenge. Serving size: 1 Lozenge, Calories 12, Total Fat 9g, Sodium 0mg, Total Carbohydrates 3.3g, Sugars 1g, Protein 0g. ZAND Herbal Formula.

SOLGAR® MULTIPLE VITAMIN, MINERAL, and HERBAL DIETARY SUPPLEMENT. *Sugar-free and Starch-free. Advanced Phytonutrient Multiple Vitamin, Mineral, and Herbal Formula for Women (Male Multiple also available). Suitable for Vegetarians.* Calories 15, Total Carbohydrate 3g, Dietary Fiber 2g, Protein 1g, up to 3333% of 25 vitamins and minerals, and 20 Essential Herbs. Manufactured by: SOLGAR VITAMIN AND HERB

TOM'S® OF MAINE NATURAL FLUOURIDE TOOTHPASTE.
No Saccharin. No Artificial Sweeteners or Preservatives. No Artificial Color or Flavor. No Animal Ingredients. Sweetened with Xylitol. Flavors: Baking Soda/Ginger Mint. Net Wt. 6 oz. (113 ml). TOM'S OF MAINE.

Packaged Dinners

WEIGHT WATCHERS® SMART ONES® FIESTA CHICKEN.
Spicy ranchero sauce with white meat chicken & spanish rice. 99% Fat-free. 2 grams of Fat. Contains Maltodextrin. Net Wt. 8.5oz. (241g), Serving Size 1 Entree, Calories 210, Calories from Fat 20, Total Fat 2g, Saturated Fat 0.5g, Polyunsaturated Fat 0.5g, Monounsaturated Fat 1g, Cholesterol 25mg, Sodium 570mg, Total Carbohydrate 35g, Dietary Fiber 5g, **Sugars 5g**, Protein 13g, Vitamin A 8%, Calcium 4%, Vitamin C 20%, Iron 6%. WEIGHT WATCHERS GOURMET FOOD CO.

WEIGHT WATCHERS® SMART ONES® LASAGNA BOLOGNESE.
Curly, bite-sized lasagna ribbons in a rich Bolognese-meat sauce with mozzarella. Net Wt. 9 oz. (255g), Serving size 1 Package, Calories 240, Calories from Fat 25, Total Fat 2.5g, Saturated Fat 1g, Polyunsaturated Fat 0.5g, Monounsaturated Fat 0.5g, Cholesterol 10mg, Sodium 560mg, Total Carbohydrate 43g, Dietary Fiber 4g, **Sugars 5g,** Protein 13g, Vitamin A 10%, Vitamin C 8%, Calcium 15%, Iron 10%. HEINZ FROZEN FOOD COMPANY.

WEIGHT WATCHERS® SMART ONES® CREAMY RIGATONI With BROCCOLI & CHICKEN. *A medley of pasta, broccoli and chicken tenderloins in a creamy Fontina Cheese sauce.* Net Wt. 9 oz. (255g), Serving size 1 Package, Calories 240, Calories from Fat 30, Total Fat 3.5g, Saturated Fat 1g, Polyunsaturated Fat 1g, Monounsaturated Fat 1g, Cholesterol 25mg, Sodium 780mg, Total Carbohydrate 39g, Dietary Fiber 4g, **Sugars 7g,** Protein 16g, Vitamin A 6%, Vitamin C 2%, Calcium 15%, Iron 10%. HEINZ FROZEN FOOD COMPANY.

WEIGHT WATCHERS® SMART ONES® SPICY SZECHUAN STYLE VEGETABLES (Noodles) & CHICKEN. 98% Fat Free. Net Wt. 9 oz. (255g), Serving size 1 Entree, Calories 230, Calorie from Fat 45, Total Fat 5g, Polyunsaturated Fat 2g, Monounsaturated Fat 2g, Cholesterol 10mg, Sodium 800mg, Total Carbohydrate 34g, Dietary Fiber 3g, **Sugars 4g,** Protein 11g, Vitamin A 6%, Vitamin C 10%, Calcium 4%. HEINZ FROZEN FOOD COMPANY.

LEAN CUISINE® CAFE CLASSICS MEAT LOAF WITH GRAVY AND WHIPPED POTATOES. Net Wt. 9 3/8 oz. (265g), Serving size 1 Package, Calories 260, Calories from Fat 60, Total Fat 7g, Saturated Fat 4g, Polyunsaturated Fat .5g, Monounsaturated Fat 2.5g, Cholesterol 45mg, Sodium 600mg, Total Carbohydrate 28g, Dietary Fiber 4g, **Sugars 5g,** Protein 20g, Vitamin A 2%, Vitamin C 0%, Calcium 8%, Iron 15%. Contains Molasses, High Fructose Corn Syrup, Sugar, Dextrose. LEAN CUISINE® PRODUCTS, NESTLE' USA FOOD GROUP, INC.

Pancake & Waffle Mix

ARROWHEAD MILLS® MULTI GRAIN PANCAKE & WAFFLE MIX
No added sugar. Good source of fiber. Organically produced grains. No additives or preservatives. No addition of eggs or milk required. Also available: Gluten-Free Pancake Mix, Buckwheat Pancake Mix, Blue Corn Pancake Mix, Oat Bran Pancake Mix. Includes recipe for fat free muffins. Net Wt. 32 oz. (2 lbs.) 907g, Serving size 1/4 cup (35g), Servings per container 26, Calories 120, Calories from Fat 5, Total Fat 0.5g, Saturated Fat 0g, Cholesterol 0mg, Sodium 280mg, Potassium 130mg, Total Carbohydrate 25g, Dietary Fiber 3g, **Sugars 2g**, Protein 4g, Vitamin A 2%, Calcium 10%, Iron 4%, Thiamin 4% Riboflavin 2%, Niacin 2%. ARROWHEAD MILLS, INC.

ARROWHEAD MILLS® BUCKWHEAT PANCAKE & WAFFLE MIX
No added sugar. Good source of fiber. Organically produced grains. No additives or preservatives. No addition of eggs or milk required. Also available: Gluten-Free Pancake Mix, Multi Grain Pancake Mix, Blue Corn Pancake Mix, Oat Bran Pancake Mix. Includes recipe for Buckwheat Crepes and Buckwheat Muffins. Net Wt. 32 oz. (2 lbs.) 907g, Serving size 1/4 cup (35g), Servings per container 26, Calories 120, Calories from Fat 5, Total Fat 0.5g, Saturated Fat 0g, Cholesterol 0mg, Sodium 280mg, Potassium 130mg, Total Carbohydrate 25g, Dietary Fiber 3g, **Sugars 2g**, Protein 4g, Vitamin A 2%, Calcium 10%, Iron 4%, Thiamin 4% Riboflavin 2%, Niacin 2%. ARROWHEAD MILLS, INC.

Pancake Syrup

ATKINS™ PANCAKE SYRUP, SUGAR FREE.
All Natural Flavors. 0 Grams of Carbs per Serving. Other syrup flavors include: Hazelnut, Chocolate, Strawberry, Cherry, Raspberry. MAPLE: Net Wt. 12 fl. oz. (355 ml), Serving Size 1/4 Cup (2 fl oz) 60 ml, Servings 6, Calories 0, Fat Calories 0, Total Fat 0, Sodium 35mg, Total Carbohydrate 0g, **Sugars 0g**, Protein 0g. Sweetened with Sucralose. ATKINS NUTRITIONALS, INC.

Pasta

A great way to buy whole grain pasta is in bulk from your health food store, but you can often find it at your local grocery store as well. If not, take this information to them and have it ordered for you. Most establishments are happy to please their customers.

This one's definitely a favorite. Look on the cover for Bernie, the "Rabbit of Approval:"

ANNIE'S® HOMEGROWN WHOLE WHEAT SHELLS & CHEDDAR. Certified Organic. *All Natural. No preservatives or chemicals added. Organic. Produced without the use of synthetic pesticides, fertilizers, or growth hormones.* Available at health food markets and grocery stores. Net Wt. 6 oz. (170g), Serving size 2/3 cup, Servings per box 2.5, Calories 270, Calories from Fat 45, Total Fat 5g, Saturated Fat 3g, Cholesterol 15mg, Sodium 530mg, Total Carbohydrate 45g, Dietary Fiber 8g, **Sugars 2g,** Protein 12g, Vitamin A 2%, Calcium 15%, Iron 15 %. ANNIES®

DEBOLES® WHOLE WHEAT SPAGHETTI STYLE PASTA. 100% Organically Grown Durum Whole Wheat Flour. Serving size 2 oz. (about 1 cup/57g), Servings per container 4, Net Wt. 8oz. (226g), Calories 210, Calories from Fat 15, Total Fat 2g, Cholesterol 0mg, Sodium 0mg, Total Carbohydrate 40g, Dietary Fiber 5g, **Sugars 2g,** Protein 9g, Iron 10%. DEBOLES NUTRITIONAL FOODS, A Subsidiary of Arrowhead Mills.

HODGSON MILL® WHOLE WHEAT SPINACH SPAGETTI. *All Natural. High in fiber. "Premium Quality Since 1882." Made from whole grain including the wheat germ and bran fiber.* Net Wt. 16 oz. (454g), Serving size 2 oz. dry (56.7g), Servings per container 8, Calories 190, Fat calories 15, Total Fat 2g, Saturated Fat 1g, Cholesterol 0mg, Sodium 25mg, Total Carbohydrate 35g, Fiber 5g, **Sugars 0g,** Protein 9g, Calcium 2%, Iron 15%, Thiamine 20%, Riboflavin 4%, Niacin 10%. HODGSON MILL, INC., WWSS.

Pasta Sauce

HUNT'S® SPAGETTI SAUCE. No Sugar Added. *Original Style Traditional. Comes in a can. Half the price of regular pasta sauce. All Natural. No Cholesterol. Low Fat. High Fiber.* Net Wt. 26 oz. (1 lb., 10 oz.) 737g, Serving size 1/2 cup (125g), Servings per container 6, Calories 45, Calories from Fat 10, Total Fat 1g, Saturated Fat 0g, Cholesterol 0mg, Sodium 570mg, Total Carbohydrate 9g, Dietary Fiber 3g, **Sugars 6g,** Protein 2g, Vitamin A 6%, Vitamin C 15%, Calcium 2%, Iron 8%. HUNT-WESSON, INC.

Rice and Rice Cakes

GOURMET HOUSE® Wild 'n Crispy RICE CAKES with Wild Rice *Fat Free. Taco flavor. "America's Wild Rice Experts."* Unsweetened. Net Wt. 1.5 oz. (44g), Serving size 3 cakes, Servings per container 5, Calories 40, Calories from Fat 0g, Total Fat 0g, Saturated Fat 0g, Cholesterol 0mg, Sodium 55mg, Total

Carbohydrate 8g, **Sugars 0g,** Protein 1g, Iron 1%. GOURMET HOUSE/Foodland Industries, MN, Inc.

SUCCESS® RICE BROWN & WILD MIX.

Instant. Time-saving Boil-in-Bag. Microwaveable. Satisfaction guaranteed. Net Wt. 4.5 oz. (127g), Serving size 2 oz (57g/about 3/4 cup), Calories 190, Calories from Fat 10, Total Fat 1g, Saturated Fat 0g, Cholesterol 0mg, Sodium 790mg, Total Carbohydrate 41g, Dietary Fiber 3g, **Sugars 1g,** Protein 6g, Vitamin A 10%, Calcium 2%, Iron 6%. RIVIANA FOODS.

Chapter 19
The Ice Cream Parlor
and the Fudge Factory

Diet foods can be found in the most unlikely places. To maintain your weight it is not necessary to give up all the food that you love. Nearly every ice cream or frozen yogurt establishment across the country has a sugar-free section. Most of these businesses have been catering to the diabetic population for years, but you do not have to be diabetic to enjoy these foods. Sugar-free eating is as much about prevention as it is about maintenance of a disease condition.

I was delighted several years ago to discover that a homemade fudge factory that catered to tourists outside the Olympic National Forest in Washington State, had sugar-free fudge. Before that time it never even occurred to me to ask if sugar-free options were available. Since then I ask wherever I go. While my husband usually prefers the regular version I have the sugar-free alternative whether it's frozen yogurt, ice cream cones, hot fudge sundae, banana split, milk shake, fudge, or gourmet chocolates. For the holidays we easily find sugar-free pies at the grocery store. Make a conscious decision today to look for and ask for the sugar-free options. Guilt free satisfaction is not a fantasy. You *can* have your ice cream, fudge, and cheesecakes and eat them too!

Chapter 20
Recipes

For information on whole food and sugar free recipe books, or how to order "fructose-sweetened" recipe books see the Resource Section at the back of this book. For dessert topping and pasta sauce see Chapter 18: Other Healthy Options.

Mango Moose Shake

1 teaspoon instant decaf coffee
1 cup soy milk
1 teaspoon sugar free hot chocolate
1/2 teaspoon carob powder
1 scoop sugar free protein powder
2 Tbsp. nonfat sugar free yogurt (dairy or soy)
1 Tbsp. nonfat ricotta cheese (optional)
1 Mango (may substitute with another fruit)
5-10 pumpkin seeds
5-10 almonds (preferably raw)
12-20 ice cubes

Peel fruit, slice, and add all basic ingredients to blender. Mix thoroughly. Add 6-8 ice cubes. Repeat adding ice up to four times, until desired thickness, blending in between and gradually increasing blender speed. Equals one large or two small smoothies.

Whole Grain Pasta Bake

1 lb. ground turkey
1/2 cup grated parmesan cheese
5 cups cooked whole wheat pasta
1 package shredded mozzarella cheese
1 jar sugar free spaghetti sauce

Brown ground turkey in a skillet; drain. Stir in cooked pasta, spaghetti sauce, and grated parmesan cheese. Spoon into 13 x 9 inch baking dish. Top with mozzarella cheese. Bake at 375 degrees for 20 minutes.

Health Nut Cereal

2 cups sugar-free or low-sugar (less than 7g) whole grain flakes, oats, or other whole cereal
1/2 sliced banana
1/4 cup raisins
1 tbsp. soynuts
1 tbsp. pumpkin seeds or sunflower seeds
1/4 cup slivered almonds
2 cups skim milk, soy, or rice milk
1 scoop sugar-free protein powder or unsweetened whey
Sweetener packet or 1/2 teaspoon honey or molasses (high in iron)

Use a wisk to mix milk and protein powder in bowl. Add cereal. Add fruit, nuts, and seeds.

Strawberry Shortcake

Sugar-free angel food cake
Sugar-free strawberry pudding or non-fat sugar-free strawberry yogurt
Sugar-free frozen or fresh sliced strawberries
Light whipped topping

Slice cake into three layers. Spoon yogurt or pudding onto each layer and add strawberries. Re-layer and frost entire cake with light creamy topping.

Rainbow Mac

1 lb. ground turkey
4 cups whole wheat pasta
Smart Balance margarine
1 can sugar-free fresh salsa
2 tbsp. nutritional yeast
1 can chili with beans
1/2 can sugar-free tomato sauce or paste
Hot spice powder or chili powder to taste
Diced tomato, yellow squash, zucchini, and onion (optional)
salt/pepper

Brown turkey in a skillet. Add cooked pasta, tomato sauce, salsa, onions, and chili with beans. Heat until onions are soft. Blend in margarine. Add vegetables last. Cook until tender but crisp. Add spices to taste. Top with nutritional yeast. Serves 6.

Mochachino Smoothie

1/2 banana
5-10 soy nuts, almonds, pumpkin seeds
1 teaspoon instant decaf coffee
1/2 packet instant sugar-free hot chocolate
1 teaspoon carob powder
1 cup skim milk, rice, or soy milk
1 tbsp. ricotta or soy cheese (optional)
1 tbsp. nonfat sugar-free coffee yogurt (dairy or soy)
16-20 ice cubes

Add all basic ingredients to blender. Mix thoroughly. Then add 6-8 ice cubes. Repeat adding ice up to four times, until desired thickness, blending in between and gradually increasing blender speed. Equals one large or two small smoothies.

S'Mores

Whole Grain Low-Sugar Graham Crackers
Health Food Store Marshmallows
Tropical Source® Chocolate Squares (See Chapter: 8 Chocolate)
All Natural Peanut Butter (No sugar or salt added)

These are best made over an open campfire, but your stove top burners will work just as well. Spread some peanut butter on a large square of graham cracker. Place a naturally sweetened chocolate square on top of that. Then, using a roasting stick, lightly brown one or two marshmallows until the inside is melted and warm. Sandwich the marshmallow between the chocolate and peanut butter half and another plain square of graham cracker. The hot marshmallow will melt the chocolate, so you have to eat it quickly. It's a camper's delight!

Peaches & Cream Cake

Sugar-free angel food cake
1 can of sugar-free or two fresh peaches (sliced)
Sugar-free pudding mix (vanilla, white chocolate, or banana)
Light whipped topping

Slice cake into 3 layers. Add pudding and peach slices. Re-layer and frost entire cake with light creamy topping.

Epilogue
Are We Our Bodies?

I adored this man, the only surgeon I considered to be a true artist. His hands worked deftly. He separated the flesh with symmetry, each hand mirroring the other. Finally, we were inside the body and his job was nearly accomplished. Her ovarian tubes had been *tied.* "Wait a minute," he said suddenly, as if he had forgotten something vitally important. I paused, holding the closing suture in my hand.

He walked around to the end of the OR table and moved into position between the patient's legs. As was common, her legs had been propped up into stirrups for the operation. This enabled the doctor to examine the position of her uterus and ovaries through her vagina during the surgery.

I watched curiously. He knelt down and placed his face near the vaginal opening. "Open the wound a little wider," he commanded. Obediently I did as he asked. "Look inside," he added, a little more enthusiastically. As I did so, he widened the vaginal opening and I realized then that I was staring right at his face. I was looking at him *through* the patient's body!

He smiled and waved. "Hello-o," he chimed with delight. The unexpectedness of this moment caused me to swoon. Not only were the surgeon's actions a surprise, but what about the woman? We had literally torn her apart and looked right through her. If not her body, then who was she?

The Mind Body Connection
For eons we have referenced the body and mind as separate entities. But in recent years, especially in the western world, we have begun to awaken to the fact that these two components of our being are actually one and the same, interconnected at a level that is beyond our comprehension. Therefore, who are we—really? Do our minds create our illness or does our physical state affect our mind?

For years I was told that my symptoms were all in my head. But, in the end, it was my diet—my biology—that was affecting my head! It was a great relief to discover this truth. Without the racing thoughts, insomnia, panic attacks, and other psychological symptoms I experienced due to poor diet, I am now able to access that most elusive of states, peace of mind. My dream is that you, the reader, may too achieve this clarity and that this new found self-empowerment will be the catalyst for the fulfillment of *your* dreams.

Stress and Weight

What is the simplest rule for stress? When you are tired—rest! It's really pretty simple. We tend to forget this and place rest low on our list of priorities. But stress can be a causal factor in many disease conditions and even excess weight gain. In *Fight Fat After Forty*, Pamela Peeke, M.D. tells us that there is now scientific evidence that links long-term stress to fat accumulation in the waist and abdomen of middle-aged women.

Therefore, if you start to feel a little frazzled, cut the work hours, reduce travel time, and eliminate errands. I have a certain limit: no more than two errands per day. Also, it is absolutely essential to have one full day of rest per week. No errands. No chores. No nothin'!

This may not be easy at first. Due to doctor's orders, I began applying this rule, and found it absolutely excruciating. I would sit with my fists clenched thinking of all the things that needed to be done. But, over time, I have found this to be some of the best advice I have ever received.

Here's another helpful hint. Our homes are full of reminders of things we need to do. Get away from the house. There are no "to-do" lists in nature. Walk the beach. Take a hike. Enjoy the sunset. Take yourself to a place where sitting still won't make you feel guilty. Plus, as we open ourselves to the harmony of nature, we become more attune with the natural harmony in our own lives.

Simple Meditation Exercises

My husband calls eastern philosophy that "Hindu-Gym-Shoe" stuff. Meditation and yoga have been proven to reduce blood pressure and relieve stress. Meditation need not be complicated. It can be as simple as the following exercises, yet still highly rewarding psychologically, physically, and even spiritually.

Between Errands. In between errands, pause for a moment to let the dust settle. Sit quietly in your car for ten to twenty minutes before moving on to the next item on your list. You'll be surprised how this lowers your stress level and brings to mind tasks and ideas that you might have otherwise forgotten.

Corpse Pose. Find a moment when you can turn the TV off and just sit, perhaps after everyone else has gone to bed. Try Corpse Pose (a simple yoga position) by just sprawling out on the floor, on your back, eyes closed, and completely relaxed. Clear your mind of all thoughts. Ten to twenty minutes is all you need.

Empty Mind. When trying to meditate, if you find yourself having some trouble clearing your mind of extraneous thoughts, you can repeat to yourself, over and over, the words *empty mind – empty mind.* Repetitive words or phrases are called mantras, chants, or prayers and are common as self-centering tools in many cultures.

Radio Off. While you are driving, turn the radio off and listen to your own thoughts for a while. Let issues resolve themselves in your mind that is now free of clutter.

Mute the Commercials or just turn your television off. Don't let TV take the place of reading, crafts, games, sports, exercise, communication, or making love! Live your life instead of observing the lives of others passively. An active life will help combat depression and "couch potato" weight gain.

Clear Your Space. Develop a habit of cleaning and organizing your space for thirty minutes to an hour every day, preferably in the morning before you start your day. A neat, well-organized living area creates a positive flow of energy (Feng Shui) throughout your environment, reducing your stress level and supporting your wellbeing and productivity.

Our home is our center, literally our foundation, and it must be our first priority. It should be a place of refuge and relaxation. Feeling good is requisite to good health. A home that is cluttered will create a subtle, yet constant sense of guilt and nagging negativity.

More Diet Help

Positive Verbal Programming. This is audio meditation, a form of self-hypnosis that utilizes the power of words as tools for self-transformation. Sound is nothing more than vibration, and vibrations (or waves) are at the very center of all life. In essence, by creating sound through the spoken word, you are creating new life.

The secret to hypnosis is that the mind responds only to positive commands. Begin to develop your own series of positive affirmations or words that you speak out loud whenever you need a boost. When you are feeling insecure, fat, and unattractive—speak these words out loud:

I am beautiful, I am slender, I am healthy and strong!

If you are depressed, not feeling well, or just generally down in the dumps you might say out loud to yourself:

I am happy, I am healthy, and I have a good, fun life!

You will be surprised at the results. Your mind will begin to make your spoken words a reality for you. Physiologically, our minds must respond to our words and our attitude. It does not matter that we do not have these things already. By focusing on our faults, needs, or inadequacies we define ourselves by a state of lack. We create a *victim* persona. Only by *imagining* that we already have the things we want, can we begin to *create them in reality*. The outer world is always a reflection of our inner world. A great philosopher once said, "What you focus on expands." That includes your waist line!

Consider this, you cannot criticize and be appreciative at the same time. By focusing on the positive (even *imaginary* positives!) we create for ourselves a world of healing, growth, and prosperity. After all, to say "I am rich" means so much more than just having money.

When all is said and done regarding our weight, we must still remember that inner beauty is the only beauty that lasts. Even if we never lost a single pound, we would still be perfect just as we are. Self-acceptance is the key to success. Here is one more affirmation to help us clarify this point:

I am accepted, I am loved, I am perfect just as I am.

A great way to affirm is while driving. If anyone sees you they will just assume that you are singing along to the radio, or you can create your own audio tape. Be sure to allow spaces between affirmations so that you can repeat them out loud.

Creative Visualization. Another way to help create a new you is through creative visualization. Remember daydreaming? They say that if you can *see* it, you can *be* it. Find a quiet place, relax, and close your eyes. Now, really *see* yourself as you would like to be. If you would like to lose some weight, *see* yourself thin. What kind of clothes are you wearing? What are you doing? How does it *feel* to be thin? That brings us to our last exercise.

Imagine and Feel. Sensory meditation helps you change your world from the inside out. The next time you notice that your outer world is less than satisfying, stop, close your eyes for a moment and imagine how it would *feel* to have exactly what you want. It doesn't matter whether it is your perfect figure, your perfect soul mate, or more money, our outer world is created by the energy generated from our inner world. We are not a reflection of our circumstances but, rather, the events of our lives are a projection outward from the energy we hold inside us! (See *Chakras for Beginners* by Dave Pond).

I read something once in a delightful little book called *The Incredible Credible Cosmic Consciousness Diet Book.* It really hit home for me and it goes something like this:

Them that loves ya' is gonna love ya' no matter what you do.
And them that don't love ya' ain't gonna love ya'
no matter what you do.

This is a perfect example of projection. You cannot convince someone that cannot be convinced, not even yourself. Believe the dream inside yourself first and the rest will follow. Oh, by the way, this quote is something to consider, too, if it is someone else that you are trying to lose weight for and not yourself.

There are some great books and tapes available about the mind body connection. A must for every health seeker is Dr. Bernie Siegel's *Love, Medicine, and Miracles.* Also read Norman Cousin's *Anatomy of an Illness,* and Dr. William Mundy's, *Curing Allergies with Visual Imagery.* Wayne Dyer is one of my favorites and Deepak Chopra, M.D., a western-trained physician with an eastern philosophy, has many books and tapes also referencing the power of the mind to create health.

Resources

Books:

-*Anatomy of an Illness: As Perceived by the Patient,* Norman Cousins, 1991, Bantam Books

-*The Crazy Makers: How the Food Industry is Destroying our Brains and Harming our Children,* Carol Simontacchi, 2000, Penguin Putnam, Inc., New York, NY, www.penguinputnam.com

-*Eating Well for Optimum Health,* Andrew Weil, M.D., 2000, Knopf/Random House, Inc., www.randomhouse.com

-*Fit for Life: A New Beginning,* Harvey Diamond, 2000, Kensington Books Corp., New York, NY, www.kensingtonbooks.com

-*Hypoglycemia: A Better Approach,* Dr. Paavo Airola, 1977/1996 Twenty-first Printing, Health Plus Publishers, Sherwood, Oregon,

-*Hypoglycemia: The Disease Your Doctor Won't Treat,* Jeraldine Saunders/Dr. Harvey M. Ross, 1980, Kensington Publishing Corp., New York, NY

-*Lick the Sugar Habit,* Nancy Appleton, 1996/97, Avery Publishing Group, Penguin Putnam, Inc.

-*Love, Medicine, & Miracles: Lessons Learned About Self-Healing From A Surgeon's Experience with Exceptional Patients,* Bernie Siegel, M.D., 1986/98, HarperCollins Publishers, Inc., New York, NY

-*The New Yoga for People Over 50,* Suza Francina, 1997, Health Communications, Inc., Deerfield Beach, FL

-*The Power of Flow: Practical Ways to Transform Your Life with Meaningful Coincidence,* Meg Lundstrom, Charlene Belitz, 1998, Three Rivers Press

-*Richard Hittleman's 28 Day Yoga Exercise Plan,* Richard L. Hittleman, 1969, Workman Publishing Co. Inc., New York, NY,

-*Stop the Insanity: Eat, Breathe, Move,* Susan Powter, Bill Grose (Editor), Pocket Books

-*Sugar Blues,* William Dufty, 1975, Warner Books, New York, NY,

-*Sugar Busters! Cut Sugar to Trim Fat,* H. Leighton Steward, et al., 1995/1998, Metairie, LA.

-*Unlimited Power: The Way to Peak Personal Achievement,* 1997, Anthony Robbins, Ballantine Books, Inc., New York, NY

-*Walk Yourself Well: Eliminate Back, Neck, Shoulder, Knee, Hip, and Other Structural Pain Forever–without Surgery or Drugs,* Sherry Brourman, P.T., 1998, Hyperion, New York, NY,

-*Yoga Journal,* P.O. Box 11684, Riverton, NJ 08076-1684, 1-800-600-YOGA, www.yogajournal.com

-*You Don't Have to be Thin to Win,* Judy Molnar/Bob Babbitt, 2000, Villard

-*Your Body's Many Cries for Water: You Are Not Sick, You Are Thirsty,* Fereydoon Batmanghelidj, Global Health Solutions, Falls Church, VA

-*The Zone: A Dietary Roadmap,* Dr. Barry Sears/Bill Lawren, 1995, Harper-Collins, New York, NY,

Recipe Books

In addition to a large assortment of books labeled *diabetic recipes,* check out these books. Also, try the cookbook section of your local library.

-*Sweet and Sugar Free:* An All-Natural Fruit-Sweetened Dessert Cookbook (includes pies, muffins, and breads), Karen E. Barkie, 1982, St. Martin's Press, New York, NY
-*Fancy, Sweet and Sugar Free* (unique dessert recipes for those special occasions), Karen E. Barkie, 1985, St. Martin's Press, New York, NY
-*No Salt, No Sugar, No Fat Cook Book,* Jacqueline Williams and Goldie Silverman, Bristol Publishing Enterprises, Inc., San Leandro, CA
-*Sugar Busters!™ Quick & Easy Cook Book* (Ring bound), H. Leighton Steward, et. al., Ballantine Books/Random House, Inc.
www.randomhouse.com, www.sugarbusters.com
-*Fruit Sweet and Sugar Free,* Janice Feuer, 1993, Healing Arts Press,
Rochester, VT, www.innertraditions.com
-*Cooking the Whole Foods Way* (as seen on Public Television), Christina Pirello, HP Books/The Berkeley Publishing Group, New York, NY
-*Starting Over: Learning to Cook with Natural Foods,* Delia Quigley and Polly Pitchford, The Book Publishing Co., Summertown, TN
-*Rodale's Basic Natural Foods Cook Book:* Over 1500 Easy-to-Follow Recipes, Charles Gerra, Editor, Rodale Press, Inc., Fireside Books, New York, NY

Recipes by Mail

To receive fructose sweetened recipes contact: TKI Foods, Inc., P.O. Box 3877, Springfield, IL, 62708–3877 with check or money order, your name and address, and the bottom panel of a box of Sweet Lite® Fructose (see Chapter 1: Natural Sweeteners).

Recipe Books include:
1. *Menu Magic with Sweetlite® Fructose,* by Jeanne Jones, A collection of delicious recipes featuring granular fructose.
2. *More Menu Magic with Sweelite® Liquid Fructose,* by Jeanne Jones, Recipes to make complete meals using liquid fructose.
3. *The Fructose Cookbook* (131 recipes), by Minuah Cannon.
4. *The Fabulous Fructose Recipe Book,* by J.T. Cooper, M.D. and Jeanne Jones.
5. *Dr. Cooper's Fabulous Fructose Diet,* by J.T. Cooper, M.D.

The Internet

www.diabeatit.com — A site developed as a resource and community for diabetics and their families.

www.vegkitchen.com — Visit Nava Atlas' web site for easy recipes and kitchen wisdom. She is the author of several vegetarian cookbooks, including *Vegetarian Express Pasta* and *East to West.*

www.diabetes.org — American Diabetes Association (ADA)
1-800-DIABETES (1-800-342-2383)
Email: membership@diabetes.org

Yahoo!News — Full Coverage—Obesity and Weight Issues, On-line Chat

www.acsm.org — American College of Sports Medicine
P.O. Box 1440, Indianapolis, IN, 46206-1440

http://gorp.com/gorp — Adventurous Traveler Bookstore/excerpts from *Medicine for the Backcountry* by Buck Tilton M.S. & Frank Hubbell, D.O.

www.cspinet.org — The Center for Science in the Public Interest, a Washington, D.C., consumer advocacy group that lis sugar consumption up by 28% since 1983.

www.healthfree.com — Stevia information.
www.holisticmed.com — Stevia information.
www.wisdomherbs.com — Stevia information.
www.steviaplus.com — Stevia information.

Bibliography

-Adler, Jerry and Claudia Kalb, *An American Epidemic: Diabetes-The Silent Killer*, Newsweek, September 4, 2000, p. 40-47.

-Airola, Dr. Paavo, *Hypoglycemia: A Better Approach*, 1977/1996 Twenty-first Printing, Health Plus Publishers, P.O. Box 1027, Sherwood, Oregon 97140.

-American Book Trade Directory, 45th Edition, R.R. Bowker's, 1999-2000.

-American Diabetes Association (ADA), 1701 N. Beauregard St., Alexandria, VA 22311.

-American Medical Association, 515 North State St., Chicago, IL. 60610, www.amer-assn.org.

-Appleton, Nancy, *Lick the Sugar Habit*, 1996/97, Avery Publishing Group.

-Atkins, Robert C., M.D., *Dr. Atkin's Diet Revolution: The High Calorie Way to Stay Thin Forever*, 1972/97, Avon.

-Austin, Elizabeth, *Think You're Eating Healthy?: Don't be so sure!*, Self Magazine, November 1999, p.146.

-Batmanghelidj, Fereydoon, *Your Body's Many Cries for Water: You Are Not sick, You are Thirsty*, Global Health Solutions, P.O. Box 3189, Falls Church, VA 22043.

-Benac, Nancy, *America's Prosperity Has Grown Since 1992*, The Bradenton Herald Tribune, Vol. 79, No. 52, November 5, 2000.

-Berger, Stuart M., M.D., *Dr. Berger's Immune Power Diet*, 1985, New American Library, 1633 Broadway, New York, NY 10019.

-Birrer, Richard, *Problems in Diabetes: Assessing and Treating Hypoglycemic Events*, Patient Care, April 30, 1999, Vol. 33, Issue 8, p. 22-40, Oradell.

-The Bowker Annual Library and Book Trade Almanac, 44th Edition, 1999.

-Budd, Martin L., *Low Blood Sugar: Coping with Low Blood Sugar (Hypoglycemia)*, 1997, Thorsons Health Series/ HarperCollins Publishers, 77–85 Fulham Palace Rd, Hammersmith, London W68JB.

-Cass, Hyla, *Get a Grip on Anxiety*, Let's Live, August 2000, Vol. 68, Issue 8, p. 72-76, Los Angeles.

-D'Arrigo, Terri, *Hypoglycemia and Driving*, Diabetes Forecast, December 1999, Vol. 52, Issue 12, p.29-30, Alexandria.

-Diamond, Harvey, *Fit for Life: A New Beginning*, 2000, Kensington Books Corp., 850 Third Ave., New York, NY 10022 www.kensingtonbooks.com.

-Diamond, Harvey and Marilyn, *Fit for Life*, 1987, Warner Books, Inc., 666 Fifth Ave., New York, NY 10103.

-The Diet Debunker, About.com, 2000.

-Dufty, William, *Sugar Blues*, 1975, Warner Books, 75 Rockefeller Plaza, New York, NY 10019.

-Eades, Michael R., M.D. and Mary Dan Eades, M.D., *Protein Power*, 1996, Bantam Books, 1540 Broadway, New York, NY 10036.

-Energy Times, *Eating, Exercising and Weight Control*, Part 1, p. 72, October 2000.

-Fitzgerald, Randy, *Sugar's Sweet Deal*, Reader's Digest, February 1998.

-Francina, Suza, *The New Yoga for People Over 50*, 1997, Health Communications, Inc., 3201 S.W. 15th st., Deerfield Beach, FL 33442.

-Fritzsching, 1995, www.isomalt.de/english.

-Grim, Michele, R.D., L.D., *Sugar Substitutes*, Natural Awakenings: The Resource Magazine for Personal and Planetary Health, July 2000, .

-Heller, Rachael F., *The Carbohydrate Addict's Diet,* 1991/1993, Signet.
-Henner, Marilu and Laura Morton, *Marilu Henner's Total Health Makeover,* 1998, HarperCollins, New York, 10022.
-*The Incredible Credible Cosmic Consciousness Diet Book,* author unknown, circa 1985
-Jacobson, Michael F., *How Much Sugar? Labels Should Say,* Nutrition Action Health Letter, September 2000, Vol. 27, Issue 7, p. 2, Washington.
-Johnson, Mary, *When "Perfect" Isn't, Case Studies: Hypoglycemia–Belligerent and Aggressive Behavior,* Diabetes Forecast, October 2000, Vol. 53, Issue 10, p. 51-52, Alexandria.
-Journal of the American Medical Association (JAMA), 10/27/00.
-Krimmel, Edward and Patricia, *The Low Blood Sugar Handbook: You Don't Have to Suffer,* Preface by Harvey M. Ross, M.D., 1992, Franklin Publishers, Bryn Mawr, PA.
-The Literary Market Place (LMP), 2000, Volume 2, Palace Press International.
-Ludwig, David, M.D., Pediatrics, March 1999, M.D., *The Effects of low, medium, and high-GI meals on the appetite levels of 12 obese teenage boys.*
-Lundstrom, Meg and Charlene Belitz, *The Power of Flow: Practical Ways to Transform Your Life with Meaningful Coincidence,* 1998, Three Rivers Press.
-MacFarlane, Muriel, R.N., M.A., *The Panic Attack, Anxiety & Phobia Solutions Handbook,* 1997, United Research Publishers, Encinitas, CA .
-Martini, Betty, *Aspartame Crisis Posed to World Environmental Conference,* www.Rense.com, August 17, 2000.
-McQuillan, Susan, Elaine Khosrova, and Edward Saltzman, *The Complete Idiot's Guide to Losing Weight,* 1998, Alpha.
-Mellin, Laurel, M.A., R.D., *The Solution: Winning Ways to Permanent Weight Loss,* 1997, HarperCollins Publishers, Inc., New York, NY.
-Messina, Mark, PhD. and Virginia Messina, R.D., *The Simple Soybean and Your Health,* 1994, Paragon Press, Honesdale, PA.
-Mitchell, Tedd, M.D., *Extinguish Your Habit for Good,* Health Smart, USA Weekend, November 3-5, 2000, p. 4.
-Molnar, Judy and Bob Babbitt, *You Don't Have to be Thin to Win,* 2000, Villard.
-Mullarkey, Barbara Alexander and Adell V. Newman, *Sweet Delusion–How Safe is Your Artificial Sweetener?, Part One: The Hidden History of Aspartame,* The Magazine of Health, Prevention, and Environmental News, May/June 1994, Vol. 1, Issue 4.
-Murphy, Dee, *Call in the Sugar Zappers!,* Current Health 2, September 2000, Highland Park.
-National Institute of Health, NIH, Bethesda, Maryland 20892, www.nih.gov.
-Nexus Magazine, Volume 2, #2 (Oct-Nov 1995), Volume 3, #1 (Dec 1995, Jan 1996), Mapleton, QLD 4560, Australia.
-Oakes, Stephanie, *FitSmart,* USA Weekend, November 3-5, 2000, p. 28.
-Ornish, Dean, M.D., *Dr. Dean Ornish's Program for Reversing Heart Disease,* 1990, Ballantine Books, Random House, Inc., New York.
-Peeke, Pamela, M.D., *Fight Fat After Forty, 2000,* Viking Press, Penguin Audio.
-Peters, Diane, *Sweet Seduction,* Chatelaine, May 2000, Toronto.
-Pond, David, *Chakras for Beginners: A Guide to Balancing Your Chakra Energies,* 1999, Llewellyn Publications, A Division of Llewellyn Worldwide, Ltd., P.O. Box 64383, Dept. K537-1, St. Paul, MN 55164-0383 www.llewellyn.com.
-Powter, Susan and Bill Grose (Editor), *Stop the Insanity: Eat, Breathe, Move,* Pocket Books.

-Pritikin, Nathan and Patrick M. McGrady, Jr., *The Pritikin Program for Diet & Exercise,* 1980, Bantam Books, Inc., New York, NY.

-*Psyching Out Diabetes: A Positive Approach to Your Negative Emotions,* 1997, Lowell House, Los Angeles, CA.

-Readers Digest Association, Inc., 1997.

-Robbins, Anthony, *Unlimited Power: The Way to Peak Personal Achievement,* 1997, Ballantine Books, Inc., New York.

-Ross, M.A., Julia, *The Diet Cure,* 1999, Penguin Putnam.

-Saunders, Jeraldine and Dr. Harvey M. Ross, *Hypoglycemia: The Disease Your Doctor Won't Treat,* 1980, Kensington Publishing Corp., New York, NY.

-Sears, Dr. Barry and Bill Lawren, *The Zone: A Dietary Roadmap,* 1995, Harper Collins, New York, NY.

-*The Shining,* 1980, Warner Studios/Warner Home Video.

-Somer, Elizabeth, R.D., *Make Your Own Happy Food: Depression Danger Zone,* Prevention Magazine, December 1999, p.124.

-Somers, Suzanne, *Wednesday's Children: Adult Survivors of Abuse Speak Out.*

-Statistical Abstract of the United States, 1999, 119th Edition.

Stevia Herb, Healthfree.com/herbgarden/stevia, p. 1-5.

-Steward, H. Leighton, et al., *Sugar Busters! Cut Sugar to Trim Fat,* 1995/1998, Metairie, LA.

-*Sweet Choices,* Diabetes Forecast, June 2000, Vol. 53, Issue 6, p. 89-90, Alexandria.

-Thompson, Mavis, M.D., *Obesity: Vital Health Information for African-Americans,* 1999, Kensington Publishing.

-Time Almanac, 1999, Information Place LLC, Time Inc./Home Entertainment.

-Utley, Michael, *Growers See Science as Ally in Sour Reply to 'Sugar Busters!',* The Palm Beach Post, August 30, 1998, p.1A.

-Weil, Andrew, M.D., *Eating Well for Optimum Health,* 2000, Knopf/Random House, Inc., www.randomhouse.com.

-Wervach, Melvyn R., M.D., *Health & Nutrition Breakthroughs,* July 1998, Does Sugar Make Kids Hyper?

-Williams, Dr. Roger J., *Nutrition Against Disease,* 1973, Pitman Publishing, 6 East 43rd St., New York, NY 10017.

-Zemel, Dr. Michael, Great Life Magazine, *Count Calcium and Calories for Weight Control, "Effects of Dietary Calcium on Adipocyte Lipid Metabolism... ",* August 2000.

Index

T-V

W-Z

Other Books From Safe Goods/New Century Publishing 2000

Curing Allergies with Visual Imagery $14.95 US
New concepts of mind/body control $ 22.95 CA

The All Natural High Performance Diet $ 7.95 US
Improve your physical, mental and sexual performance $ 11.95 CA

Velvet Antler $ 9.95 US
Nature's Superior Tonic $ 14.95 CA

A Doctor in Your Suitcase $ 7.95 US
Natural medicine for self care when you are away from home. $ 11.95 CA

Self-Care Anywhere $19.95 US
Powerful natural remedies for common health ailments. $ 29.95 CA

Overcoming Senior Moments $ 7.95 US
Evaporating thoughts – cause and treatment $11.95 CA

Cancer Disarmed $ 4.95 US
How cancer works and what can disarm it. $ 6.95 CA

Nutritional Leverage for Great Golf $ 9.95 US
How to improve your score on the back nine $14.95 CA

The Fitness for Golfers Handbook $14.95 US
Taking your golf game to the next level. $ 19.95 CA

To order contact:
(877) 742-7078 toll free
(905) 471-5711